Manatees
and
Dugongs

MANATEES
AND
DUGONGS

John E. Reynolds III
and
Daniel K. Odell

Facts On File
New York • Oxford

Manatees and Dugongs
Copyright © 1991 by John E. Reynolds III and Daniel K. Odell

Facts On File, Inc.
460 Park Avenue South
New York NY 10016
USA

Facts On File Limited
Collins Street
Oxford OX4 1XJ
United Kingdom

Library of Congress Cataloging-in-Publication Data
Reynolds, John Elliott, 1952-
Manatees and dugongs / John Reynolds and Daniel Odell.
    p. cm.
    ISBN 0-8160-2436-7
1. Manatees. 2. Dugong.   I. Odell, Daniel K. II. Title.
    QL737.S63R49   1991
    599.5 '5—dc20   89-71399

A British CIP catalogue record for this book is available from the British Library.

Facts On File books are available at special discounts when purchased in bulk quantities for businesses, associations, institutions or sales promotions. Please contact our Special Sales Department in New York at 212/683-2244 (dial 800/322-8755 except in NY, AK, or HI) or in Oxford at 865/728399.

Text design by Donna Sinisgalli
Jacket design by Catherine Hyman
Composition by Facts On File, Inc.
Manufactured by R.R. Donnelley & Sons
Printed in the United States of America

10 9 8 7 6 5 4 3 2 1

This book is printed on acid-free paper.

W e dedicate
this book to two pioneers
in the study of sirenians,
Joseph Curtis Moore and
Daniel S. Hartman, as well
as to all scientists, past and
present, around the world
who have contributed to
increased understanding or
protection of sirenians.

CONTENTS

ACKNOWLEDGMENTS

A number of people contributed to this book. The authors appreciate comments on the text made by their colleagues: Thomas O'Shea, Lynn Lefebvre and Cathy Beck of the U.S. Fish and Wildlife Service, Bruce Ackerman of the Florida Department of Natural Resources and James Powell of Wildlife Conservation International. Eckerd College student Kim Fagan commented on a few chapters. Daryl Domning of Howard University, William A. Szelistowski of Eckerd College and Thomas O'Shea deserve particular thanks for reading and commenting on the entire text, and James Powell also merits special thanks for providing many comments and unpublished observations for inclusion in the West African manatee chapter.

Others also were helpful in providing information. The U.S. Fish and Wildlife Service's Sirenia Project in Gainesville, Florida, allowed Reynolds to peruse their files. Karl Kranz (Philadelphia Zoological Park) permitted use of his unpublished field notes on manatees in Liberia, and made some useful observations by telephone. Thomas Carr provided useful information on manatees in Angola. Michael Gosliner and David Laist of the Marine Mammal Commission described the international status (CITES and IUCN) of sirenians. The Marine Mammal Commission's executive director, John Twiss, and Daryl Domning graciously permitted the use of Domning's fine manuscript on saving sirenians as the last chapter of the book.

The authors also are grateful to people or agencies and organizations who provided slides for use in the book. Those individuals or groups were: Daryl Domning; Florida Power & Light Company; Helene Marsh; Thomas O'Shea; James Powell; Patrick Rose; Miami Seaquarium; William Szelistowski; Florida Department of Natural Resources; Anthony Preen; Paul Anderson; Great Barrier Reef Marine Park Authority; Rick Barongi; and the U.S. Fish and Wildlife Service National Ecology Research Center (Sirenia Project, Gainesville, Florida). The graphics used in the book were created by Leslie Ward and Marya Willis. Graphs were provided by the Marine Mammal Group of the Florida Department of Natural Resources. David Williams and Alice Monroe photographed lithographs, artifacts and posters for use in this book.

Finally, the authors are grateful to Roberta Dimouro of Eckerd College, who typed much of the text through various drafts, and to Facts On File senior editor Deirdre Mullane, for her encouragement and support.

INTRODUCTION

U ntil fairly recently, the three living species of manatees and the dugong were the "forgotten" marine mammals. Other marine mammals have received considerable attention. Dolphins, for example, are considered playful and intelligent, the great whales are imposing and awe-inspiring, baby harp seals make people want to hug them, and sea lions exhibit interesting territorial behavior and are familiar trained animals. The manatees and the dugong (collectively called sirenians) have, until recent decades, avoided the limelight.

Yet this seems an especially appropriate time to write a book about manatees and dugongs and about the urgent need for more protection for these species and their habitats. For example, the latest mortality figures for the Florida manatee have appeared, and they are alarming: In 1989, 174 manatees were found dead, a number significantly greater than in any previous year. The number of manatees killed by human activities in 1989 exceeded any previous peak, with 51 animals bearing irrefutable signs of being killed by boats or barges. As 1990 began, the situation worsened, with a record cold spell in Florida contributing to the deaths of nearly 60 manatees in the first two weeks of the new year. Between January 1, 1989, and May 31, 1990, 300 dead manatees were recovered in the southeastern United States. The total mortality for 1990 wound up at the unprecedented level of 216 manatees. Tragically, the United States manatee population is now thought to number slightly in excess of 1,400.

The future of the Florida manatee is precarious in the face of such high natural and human-related mortality, with an increasing number of people using our waterways and the cumulative effects of habitat destruction. Yet, the Florida manatee is not the only member of its group that has an uncertain future. Indeed, all species of sirenians are considered to be either endangered or threatened and all face hazards associated with humans. Historically, the large size, delicious meat and gentle demeanor of the sirenians made them a favorite meal for native people and explorers. Hunters harvest dugongs in

Australia, Papua New Guinea and other parts of their range; Amazonian manatees are captured and eaten in the Amazon River basin; villagers in Senegal, the Ivory Coast and other countries occasionally take West African manatees; and the West Indian manatee (the species that includes the Florida manatee) is not only consumed by people in Central and South America, but also is occasionally poached and eaten even in Florida. Just as this harvest affects all sirenian species, so does habitat destruction. One needs only to read the newspaper to discover that rain forests, seagrass meadows, coral reefs and other habitats that support sirenians worldwide continue to disappear. In addition to outright habitat destruction, humans modify habitat by introducing pollutants and exotic species.

Human activities may jeopardize the survival of sirenians, but the opposite is not true. The sirenians are unaggressive herbivores that spend their days consuming vast quantities of vegetation, occasionally interacting with other members of their kind, resting or simply traveling and exploring. Although Florida manatees can exceed 3,500 pounds in weight, they and their slightly smaller relatives are harmless to people.

Early scientists may not have studied the sirenians closely, but others knew of their existence and referred to them in various accounts. The name of the group, Sirenia, recalls sirens, the mythical mermaids that tried vainly to lure the ancient Greek hero Odysseus and his crew onto jagged rocks in the *Odyssey*. Hundreds of years ago, mariners believed that manatees and dugongs were indeed the mermaids of legend, and Christopher Columbus allegedly spotted some manatees (which might actually have been Caribbean monk seals) in 1493; he recorded in his log that the "mermaids" were not quite as lovely as he had been led to believe. The explorer, William Bartram, described manatees and manatee hunting in Florida in 1774, although he never personally saw one. Other explorers, missionaries and hunters have noted the existence and exploitation of sirenians around the world.

One of the earliest nonscientific works to mention a sirenian was Rudyard Kipling's "The White Seal." This short story romantically describes the search by a young fur seal for a place where he would be safe from sealers in the Bering Sea. He was told to look for the wise sea cow (another common name for manatees and dugongs) for advice. In the end, the seal found the sea cows and was shown a safe place for himself and other seals to live. The great irony of the story is that Kipling's wise sea cow, who discovered a refuge from hunters and graciously shared it with another beleaguered species, was, in reality, a sirenian called Steller's sea cow, which was exterminated by Russian hunters and explorers by 1768, nearly 100 years before Kipling's birth.

To understand the sirenians, one must consider at least three factors: the biology of the species, including habitat, physiology, reproduction and other

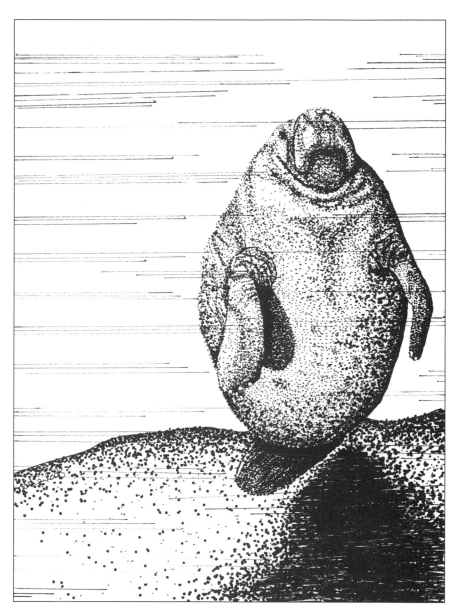

It is hard to imagine that a manatee could be confused with a mermaid. Yet the order to which the manatees and dugong belong, the Sirenia, is named for the sirens of legend. Drawing by Leslie Ward

factors; the place the sirenians occupy in certain coastal or riverine ecosystems; and the relationship that the sirenians and their ecosystems have had, and continue to have, with people. This volume provides information in all three areas.

In addition, this book is meant to tell something about humans, namely that we have immense potential, which can be used positively or negatively. The history of human interactions with most wildlife, including sirenians, has been limited to exploitation of the animals or the habitat they need to survive. The time has come when the potential for people to take positive actions must be realized. Although some difficult choices must be made, people can regulate their activities in such a way that wildlife is spared. The eminent marine mammal scientist, Kenneth S. Norris, wrote that the term "wildlife management" is a terrible misnomer; what we really mean is an attempt to manage human activities. Norris states that it is a case of human arrogance to discuss management of a species and ignore the fact that if we managed ourselves, many species would probably do just fine. The animal can not change its biology and ecology, but people can change their impact on both.

Those who would help the manatee and dugong survive face a difficult challenge for at least three major reasons:

- Sirenians breed very slowly, so depleted populations will have trouble recovering;
- For sirenians in most places in the world, scientists still lack sufficient data regarding population sizes, causes of mortality (including those associated with human activities), birthrate, seasonal distribution and habitat requirements; and
- People use the same areas that sirenians need to survive. Activities such as fishing, boating, coastal development and logging all alter habitat, but there is intense economic and political pressure to continue such activities in a poorly regulated fashion, despite the costs in both short- and long-term losses of natural resources.

We hope that readers of this book will come to understand something of the biology, ecology and behavior of the four living sirenian species and to realize the jeopardy that exists to the survival of each. Our subsequent hope is that readers will choose to support organizations (listed at the back of this volume), laws and activities whose goal is to ensure that sirenians will continue to exist for all time. Conservation of sirenians must be taken seriously immediately, or this book may one day be viewed as we view Kipling's "The White Seal"—a tale with a lesson that people learned too late.

Manatees
and
Dugongs

THE EVOLUTION OF MANATEES AND DUGONGS

Manatees and dugongs are marine mammals, like whales, dolphins, seals, sea lions and walruses. Some scientists as recently as the 19th century considered the manatee to be an unusual, tropical form of walrus; in fact, the walrus was once placed in the genus *Trichechus* along with the manatees. Despite similarities in body shape, adaptations and habitat, the manatees and dugongs (which constitute the order Sirenia) have no evolutionary relationship with other major groups of living marine mammals, which are included in the order Cetacea (whales, dolphins and porpoises) and the order Carnivora (suborder Pinnipedia—the seals, sea lions and walrus; family Mustelidae—the sea otter; and family Ursidae—the polar bear). In fact,

In this early 19th-century lithograph, the walrus (bottom right) and manatee (bottom left) are listed as members of the same genus. The other animals on the print are pinnipeds—animals normally grouped with walruses but not with sirenians. Photograph by David Williams

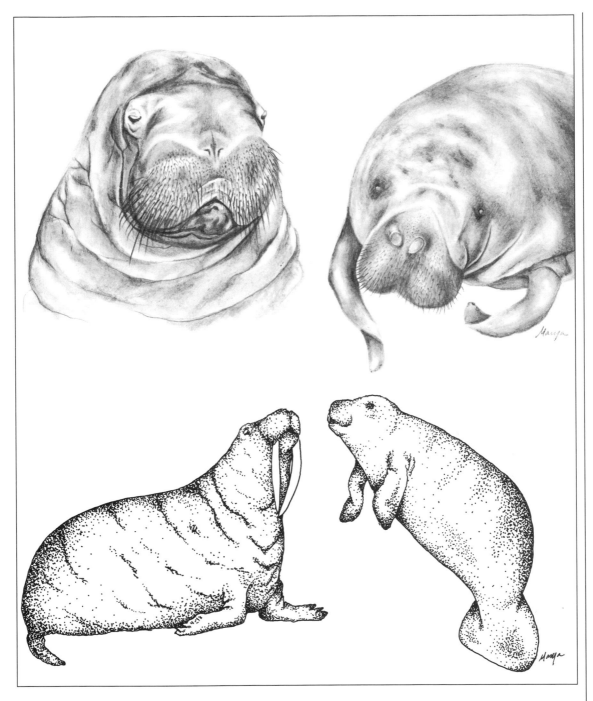

Although anatomists and zoologists 200 years ago considered manatees and walruses to be related, their physical similarities are restricted to their faces. The bodies, habitats and ancestry of the two are quite different. Drawings by Marya Willis

looking at the sirenians, one would be hard-pressed to guess the types of animals with which they have a close relationship.

The sirenians represent one of four extant orders of mammals that are sometimes lumped together as "subungulates," a series of orders that may be regarded as unusual evolutionary offshoots of a primitive ungulate ancestral stock. The other subungulates include the orders Proboscidea (elephants), Hyracoidea (hyraxes—small furry mammals that superficially resemble rodents) and Tubulidentata (aardvarks). A composite photograph showing members of these four groups does little to reinforce their relationship, but studies using biochemical analysis of proteins support a common ancestry. Certain anatomical features shared by most subungulates include dental characteristics, lack of a clavicle (collar bone) and the presence of nails or hooves, rather than primitive claws. All subungulates except the ant and termite eating aardvark are herbivorous.

The two groups of mammals whose affinity to sirenians is most frequently noted are the elephants and an extinct group called desmostylians. Subungulates like the sirenians, the desmostylians were herbivorous, hippopotamuslike mammals that appear in the fossil record from the North Pacific and represent the only extinct order of marine mammals; they lived during the Oligocene and Miocene epochs, from about 5 million to 35 million years ago.

Like the desmostylians, the sirenians reached their peak in diversity during the Oligocene and Miocene epochs, but they are an older group than the desmostylians, with ancestral forms dating from the early Eocene epoch, about 55 million years ago. The sirenians also differ from the desmostylians by having living representatives: three species of manatees and one species of dugong. Another sirenian, Steller's sea cow, survived until 1768, when it was exterminated by Russian hunters; because it existed so recently, we consider its ancestry together with the extant species.

The traits that unite the various living sirenian species include a streamlined, fusiform (literally, spindle-shaped) body that externally lacks pelvic appendages and has reduced pectoral appendages called flippers; a large, laterally expanded tail for locomotion; bones that are pachyostotic (thick or swollen), osteosclerotic (very hard and solid), and quite heavy; lack of an externally distinct neck; a relatively small brain (for animals with such large bodies) and cranial cavity; specialized dentition (teeth); the presence in most species of horny plates in the mouth to aid in crushing ingested plant materials; very sparse body hair; and large body size. (The appearance and adaptations of each sirenian species are considered in more detail in the following chapters.)

The piecing together of the sirenian ancestral puzzle has taken considerable time, patience and expertise. Much of the information that follows has

The aardvark (top), hyrax (bottom), elephant and manatee, all sub-ungulates, are related despite their very different physical appearance. Photographs by Rick Barongi

been gathered by Howard University's Daryl P. Domning, the world's foremost expert on sirenian evolution, and his colleagues around the world.

THE MANATEES—FAMILY TRICHECHIDAE

The three existing manatees are the West Indian manatee (*Trichechus manatus*), the Amazonian manatee (*Trichechus inunguis*) and the West African manatee (*Trichechus senegalensis*). The West Indian species has been differentiated using anatomical features and current distribution into two subspecies: the Florida manatee and the Antillean manatee.

Sirenian evolution is not fully understood, but it is likely that sirenians originated in the Old World (Eurasia and/or Africa), despite the fact that the oldest known fossils come from Jamaica. Within a few million years of their first appearance (i.e., in the middle Eocene, 45 million to 50 million years ago), the sirenians were represented by several genera, and they were as completely aquatic as modern species are, even though they were somewhat different in appearance. The various early sirenians spread into new regions, and it is thought that the ancestors of the manatees reached South America during this period.

CLASSIFICATION OF MODERN SIRENIANS AND RELATIONSHIP WITH OTHER MARINE MAMMALS

Phylum Chordata

  Subphylum Vertebrata

   Class Mammalia

    Order Sirenia (manatees and dugongs)

     Family Trichechidae (manatees)

      Genus and species   *Trichechus manatus* (West Indian manatee)[*]
                       Trichechus inunguis (Amazonian manatee)
                       Trichechus senegalensis (West African manatee)

     Family Dugongidae (dugongs and sea cow)

      Genus and species   *Dugong dugon* (dugong)
                       Hydrodamalis gigas (extinct Steller's sea cow)

    Order Cetacea (whales, dolphins, porpoises)

     Several Families of Cetaceans

    Order Carnivora (meat eaters)

     Suborder Pinnipedia
      Three families of seals, sea lions, walruses

      Family Mustelidae (sea otter)

      Family Ursidae (polar bear)

[*]There are two subspecies: *Trichechus manatus latirostris* (the Florida manatee)
                       Trichechus manatus manatus (the Antillean manatee)

The earliest animal that had a truly manateelike appearance, called *Potamosiren*, dates from the Miocene epoch, about 15 million years ago. Although *Potamosiren* resembled modern manatees in some regards, it lacked the extra teeth and tooth replacement characteristic of today's manatees as an adaptation for eating very abrasive plant materials. After the middle Miocene, the trichechids (manatees and manateelike animals) developed the modern-type dentition.

By the early Pliocene epoch (about 5 million years ago), some trichechids were isolated in the Amazon basin, while others had migrated into the Caribbean and reached North America. The trichechids that remained in the Amazon basin gave rise to the modern Amazonian manatee. The animals that invaded the Caribbean may have outcompeted and thereby contributed to the demise of dugongids (dugonglike sirenians) that already occupied that region (described below). In any event, the extinction of dugongs and the arrival of manatees in the Caribbean and western Atlantic occurred at roughly the same time.

The manatees that successfully invaded the Caribbean gave rise to two modern species—the West Indian and the West African manatees. The evolution of the second species is thought to have occurred due to chance colonization of Africa by animals dispersing from the Caribbean region.

THE DUGONG—FAMILY DUGONGIDAE

Although there is only one species of dugong (*Dugong dugon*) alive today, sirenians that resembled and were ancestral to the modern dugong are the most common representatives of their order in the fossil record. Not only were these dugonglike animals (called dugongids) diverse and successful, but they were also widely distributed, as early as the Eocene. Fossil remains of dugongids have been found in deposits in the Mediterranean region (from Spain to Egypt), western Europe, the southeastern United States, the Caribbean Sea, the Indian Ocean, South America and the North Pacific. It is interesting to note that sirenian fossils are often found on land, because many regions (such as Florida) that were once covered by water are now exposed.

During the Miocene (5 million to 25 million years ago), tropical conditions were widespread, coinciding with a peak in sirenian diversity and abundance. The most widespread genus was *Metaxytherium*, which is known to have passed through the Central American seaway to the Pacific Ocean, and subsequently to have occupied coastal Peru. *Metaxytherium* is considered to have given rise to a new subfamily of dugongids, which included the now extinct Steller's sea cow.

Little else is known about the ancestry of the dugong. This lack of understanding is somewhat ironic because the dugong is the most abundant and widespread species of sirenian today.

STELLER'S SEA COW—FAMILY DUGONGIDAE

Steller's sea cow (*Hydrodamalis gigas*) was bizarre looking, even for a sirenian. It was a gigantic animal, measuring at least 8 meters (25 feet) in length and estimated by different scientists to weigh between 4 and 10 metric tons. Although most other sirenians were in the past and are today tropical or subtropical, it occupied cold waters near islands in the Bering Sea. Anatomically, the sea cow was unusual because it lacked teeth and finger bones and possessed a thick, barklike skin. Accounts suggest it was also unable to dive.

The ancestry of this unusual creature has been painstakingly elaborated by Domning and his colleagues. Following the occupation of Peruvian waters by *Metaxytherium* in the Miocene epoch, sirenians began to spread northward. Fossils 10 million to 12 million years old were found in California and belonged to a species named *Dusisiren jordani*. This species was larger than typical dugongids, and had a less downturned snout and no tusks (present in the modern dugong); these characteristics suggest ancestry to Steller's sea cow. However, unlike the sea cow, *Dusisiren jordani* had teeth and finger bones. In 1986, sirenian fossils in Japan were identified as *Dusisiren dewana*, the "Great Yamagata Sea Cow," which lived about 9 million years ago and which showed reduction of its teeth and finger bones, and alteration of the wrist bones. Presumably, the Great Yamagata Sea Cow was intermediate between *Dusisiren jordani* and Steller's sea cow. A final stage before the latter appeared was *Hydrodamalis cuestae*, represented by 3-million- to 8-million-year-old fossils from California. *Hydrodamalis cuestae* lacked teeth, probably lacked finger bones and was very large. In fact, partial skulls of *Hydrodamalis cuestae* indicate that this species may have measured well over 9 meters (30 feet) long, making it even larger than Steller's sea cow.

The difficult process of determining the lineage of Steller's sea cow provides scientists with an interesting example of the various stages of the evolution of a modern marine mammal species. Sirenian fossils continue to appear, so gaps that exist in our understanding of the ancestry of other sirenians may one day be filled. Particularly in the Miocene epoch, but today as well, sirenians were important herbivores in aquatic ecosystems. Therefore, enhanced understanding of sirenian evolution should produce an additional benefit: We may gain further insight into the evolution of certain aquatic plants or plant communities.

SIGNIFICANCE OF SIRENIAN EVOLUTION ON SEAGRASSES AND OTHER AQUATIC PLANTS

Picture a group of Steller's sea cows, with each animal weighing 4 to 10 metric tons (9,000 kilograms), as it descended to graze on a bed of kelp, a large brown alga. The impact on local kelp density and distribution would be enormous, perhaps similar in impact to a herd of elephants feeding on a copse of scrub trees in Africa. When manatees in Florida aggregate at warm water outlets to escape from cold weather in winter, they too can have a measurable impact on nearby aquatic vegetation. It is possible that a very large adult manatee can consume over 90 kilograms (200 pounds) of vegetation (wet weight) each day, and winter aggregations of over 275 manatees have been sighted near several warm water refuges.

As noted, sirenians are far less abundant and diverse today (or recently) than at times in their past history (primarily in the Miocene and Oligocene epochs). If the remnant groups of sirenians that exist today can have an impact on seagrasses and other aquatic vegetation, it seems reasonable to assume that even greater potential for impact by sirenians on aquatic vegetation existed in the past.

The study of ecological relationships in the past is called paleoecology. In the Miocene fossil record from the North Pacific, for example, there have been found kelps, kelp-eating sirenians, sea urchins and marine mammals that possibly preyed on sea urchins. Kelp abundance, distribution and productivity have been clearly related to the intensity of predation on kelps by sea urchins. There exists a possibility that the kelp-eating sirenians (notably *Dusisiren* and *Hydrodamalis*) also could have subjected shallow kelp beds to significant herbivory (plant eating), thereby helping to define the nature and productivity of shallow North Pacific environments.

A GLANCE FROM PAST TO FUTURE

The sirenians enjoyed their peak in diversity and abundance millions of years ago. Today there remain only four species. What caused the decline of the sirenians? Nobody knows for certain, but a combination of climatic changes, changes in quality and/or abundance of aquatic plants for food, or competition, both with other sirenians and with other herbivores, may have contributed.

About 4 million years ago, the genus *Homo* evolved. Primitive tribes hunted and continue to hunt sirenians for food and other purposes; the slow, unaggressive, huge animals provided considerable meat, leather, fat and other products for the successful hunter. To our knowledge, however, no sirenian genus succumbed completely to the effects of primitive hunting although certain local *Hydrodamalis* stocks of Asia and North America did disappear as victims of hunting. Unfortunately, the same can not be said of more advanced societies and their impact on sirenians. As described above, Steller's sea cow was discovered by shipwrecked Russian hunters in 1741, at which time about 2,000 sea cows are thought to have existed. Twenty-seven years later, the species was extinct.

Direct hunting, therefore, can eliminate sirenian species. So, too, can habitat degradation or accidental killing of animals as a by-product of human activities. In Florida, the human population expands daily at a rate of about 1,000 new residents. The current human population of Florida already accidentally kills tens of manatees annually due to watercraft collisions, entanglement in fishing gear or crushing and drowning in canal locks or flood control structures. In a similar vein, an average of about 300 square kilometers (about 72,000 acres) of wetlands was destroyed in Florida each year between 1950 and the mid-1970s. It is not difficult to guess what the cumulative impact of such mortality or such habitat destruction is, nor to foresee how much more

Despite the high mortality and injury to manatees by watercraft, occasionally a manatee may be observed nuzzling a boat propeller. Drawing by Marya Willis

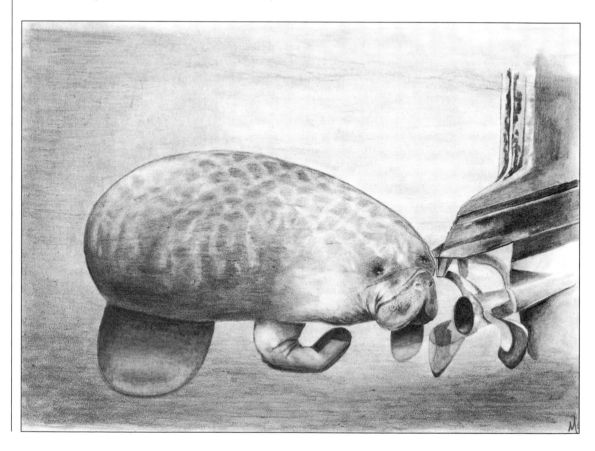

serious the impact will be as more and more people utilize dwindling space and natural resources. The same principle holds true for other living sirenians, as rain forests are decimated, fishing activity intensifies or, simply, more people use and affect waterways.

If appropriate steps are not taken soon, the effect of human activities could mean the final phase of sirenian evolution: their extinction. Extinction, *per se*, is not unnatural; but extinction that could have been, but was not, prevented is inexcusable. Since human activity currently affects sirenians in a variety of ways, it is safe to say that the long-term existence of the few remaining species is directly in our hands.

PEOPLE,
MANATEES
AND
DUGONGS

Surveys can reveal a lot about people. Not so long ago, in the mid-1970s, a survey designed to determine what people thought about manatees in Florida elicited a variety of comments that demonstrates considerable diversity and misconception.

The comments include:

"They are so ugly they're cute."

"They are a kind of insect that eats other insects" (as in the "praying manatee").

"They sure are good to eat."

"It's too bad they are going extinct."

"They don't belong in Florida since they were imported long ago, so it does not matter whether they are destroyed here."

"Keep away from them, because they are terribly dangerous."

"What's a manatee?"

Education about manatees in the United States has reduced the level of misinformation, but it has not eliminated differences among people with different priorities for use of natural resources. Thus, even today, opinions vary regarding how manatees should be treated.

A consistent feature of human interaction with all sirenians, including the manatee in Florida, is exploitation. Manatees and dugongs have been harvested for a variety of products, and their habitat has been usurped in the name of progress. Only in rare instances have human activities actually provided some benefit for the animals. In this chapter, the importance of particular sirenian species to specific cultures is briefly considered, including various ways that people around the world have trapped or harvested sirenians, the uses that have been made of parts of the animals, the massive commercial harvest of Amazonian manatees that occurred in the first half of this century and the accidental (incidental) harvest of sirenians that still occurs. (Information, where available, on specific causes of natural and human-related mortality today appears in the chapters on particular species.) Finally, we discuss cheerier topics: benign uses of sirenians, primarily as potential weed-clearing agents to eradicate mosquitoes, and a couple of human activities in Florida that have actually provided some benefit to manatees living there.

MYTHS, LEGENDS AND TRADITION

The best-known myth about the sirenians is that they are mermaids. Although it is extremely difficult to see the resemblance between a manatee or a dugong and these fabled creatures, the connection between sirenians and mermaids has persisted through time. But one must wonder what started the story in the first place. Perhaps the presence of upper body mammary glands (though they are located in the axilla or armpit), or the close association between a presumably doting mother and her calf caused the connection to be made. Perhaps someone observed a sirenian with seaweed on its head, and mistook the vegetation for hair.

However it started, the mermaid legend is harmless to manatees; in fact, it may endear them to some people. This is not the case, however, with other stories. For example, unaggressive and virtually harmless sirenians may be mistakenly considered dangerous to people. In parts of Florida, some fishermen have claimed that manatees are ferocious beasts that will steal their fish. Such people may not themselves injure manatees, but they generally do not step forward to support manatee protection.

In Cameroon, West Africa, Melissa M. Grigione, a student at Yale University, recorded some interesting superstitions and observations about manatees among villagers in the late 1980s. Fishermen in Akwen considered West African manatees dangerous and believed they could drown people. They also thought the manatees lived in caves in the river. Vice-chief Ayuketa James of the village of Egbekaw stated that manatees were dangerous and not easy to kill, and it was not worth risking one's life to eat one. In the village of Akpasang, a manatee hunter and fisherman named Joseph stated that West African manatees received power from the devil. If a person killed a manatee, Joseph asserted, the animal punished the hunter's family—unless the hunter had undergone special, traditional manatee hunting training (a prudent belief for a manatee hunter interested in monopolizing manatee capture for a village to encourage!). Although erroneous in some cases, beliefs such as these tend to prevent excessive hunting of manatees by Cameroonians.

In parts of the world, the harvest of sirenians is associated with certain traditional celebrations, and heightened stature within the community is a reward for the successful hunter. Among the native groups for whom the hunt is meaningful for cultural reasons are the Kiwai of Papua New Guinea. A documentary produced by the Australian Broadcasting Company describes the way in which the Kiwai hunt dugongs, as well as the feelings of the villagers toward their prey. For the Kiwai, the dugong hunt is an exciting and sometimes dangerous adventure, but when their quarry lies dead, the Kiwai become solemn and reverent. The documentary provides viewers with some insight as to why certain subsistence-level hunting, including hunting of rare or endangered species, can be so important to a particular people.

A number of tribes in Papua New Guinea pass on legends regarding the origin of the dugong. Kiwai legend, for example, holds that the dugong is related to the echidna or spiny anteater, citing the similarity between dugong whiskers and echidna spines. The Kilenge people believe that the dugong was originally a wild pig, that underwent a transformation. The people of the Arawe Islands tell a different story, which Brydget Hudson, former dugong project supervisor in the area has related as follows:

> One day a boy called Kasukau and his sister called Au, who lived on one of the Arawe Islands, decided to go to the mainland for water . . . When they were half way to the island a big storm blew up and the canoe almost capsized. To save his sister, the boy told her to give him his spear, net and water container. She did so, and he jumped into the water and told her to go back to the village. When he had said this, the boy turned into a dugong, and called to his sister, "If you want to come and catch me, your people must go to the mountain called Lolo and there collect the fibre from the trees to make nets such as the one I have with me. They must put the net into the water and do this very quietly or I will run away. If they catch me and bring me back to the village the women must pay for me."

This story has a number of variations; in most versions the dugong ancestor is female. These tales often provide not only an explanation of the origin of the dugong, but also of some local customs regarding its capture.

HUNTING THE SIRENIANS

The various species of sirenians have faced hunting pressure of at least three kinds: subsistence hunting, in which the hunter and his family or tribe use the meat, hide or other products themselves; commercial hunting, in which the hunter sells his catch, or parts thereof; and incidental take, in which the sirenian is not the target of the hunter, but rather is harvested during some other activity such as netting fish. Even where the take of sirenians is incidental, the hunter or fisherman will use the carcass.

Sirenians may also be taken incidental to activities besides fishing or hunting and the meat and other products are not used, except possibly by scientists wishing to learn about the animals. Examples of this particularly wasteful sort of incidental take involve dugongs in Queensland, Australia being entangled and drowned in nets placed along beaches to protect swimmers from sharks, and manatees in Florida being mutilated or killed as a result of frequent collisions with watercraft. In addition, flood control structures kill manatees in Florida, as do salinity dams in Senegal and hydroelectric dams in Nigeria.

The sirenians are all large animals, and they are sought primarily for their meat. Oddly enough, the meat can be different colors in different regions of the body due to different amounts of a protein called myoglobin and can apparently taste differently as well (some muscle tasting like veal, other areas

Florida manatee with scars inflicted by a boat's propeller. Drawing by Leslie Ward

like pork or beef), so a connoisseur could enjoy a variety of dishes from one animal.

The thick hide can be made into a variety of products such as shields, whips and other durable leather goods. The bones, such as the ribs, are thick and heavy, making them useful as weapons or for carving. The fat of the animals has been used for cooking or medicine. And the tears, especially of the dugong, have been alleged to have aphrodisiac qualities.

Hunters of sirenians use parts from the animals in similar ways. However, the way in which hunting is done, as well as the magnitude and impact of that hunting on local sirenian populations, has differed around the world.

Historical records and the presence of bones in archeological digs suggest that the West Indian manatee was once common enough in many parts of its range (along the Atlantic coasts of southern North and northern South America) to be at least an important supplement, if not a staple, of the diet. In at least some locations, such as Honduras, the once abundant species is now greatly reduced in numbers, and hunting is likely to have played a major part in the reduction. Hunting by native people certainly accounted for some of the take of manatees. From the 16th century, Mayans in Mexico and Miskito Indians in Nicaragua struck manatees with harpoons to which a rope and a floating buoy were attached (a method still used in some locations today). The

Miskito Indians, at least, pursued their prey and killed it by clubbing its head, whereas the Mayans apparently just dragged the animal ashore after it died from its wounds. Guiana Indians in northeastern South America sometimes caught manatees using bait: a moku-moku flower suspended just over the surface of the water. As the manatee stretched upward to reach the flower it was shot with arrows.

Early buccaneers and explorers played an important role in reducing the herds as well. From the 1600s, for example, there are accounts of buccaneers killing manatees around Bahia Almirante and Bocas del Toro, in the Republic of Panama, and provisioning their boats with the meat. Manatees are very rare in this area today. In Cuba, manatees were captured in the 16th century both by Indians, who used tethered remoras (suckerfish) to find and secure manatees, and by Spaniards who used crossbows. Hunting of West Indian manatees still occurs, at undetermined levels, in many Caribbean and Central and South American countries today.

In Florida, there is archeological evidence that manatees have been hunted since the Paleo-Indian period (8500–6000 B.C.). This time period coincides with the earliest known occupation of Florida by aboriginal Indians. Not surprisingly, most of the manatee remains recovered from archeological sites come from coastal and inland riverine areas, but manatee bones in habitation middens (refuse heaps) are rare. One theory advanced to explain this is that hunters ambushed manatees at predictable locations along waterways and butchered the animals where they were killed. The useless parts of the carcass, including some of the heavy bones, might have been left behind, with the hunters carrying only the most worthwhile parts back to their dwellings.

Another explanation for the rarity of manatee bones in ancient habitation middens is that the early occupants of Florida simply did not hunt manatees to a great extent. Sandra Peterson, who has studied human interactions with manatees in Florida, felt that the large mammals were probably very difficult for primitive Indians to capture and kill, due to their sensitive hearing, large size, thick skin, wary behavior and dispersed distribution during much of the year. Peterson indicates that the majority of archeological sites where manatee parts have been found coincide with springs and other warm water sources; at such sites, manatees would aggregate in winter to avoid the harmful effects of cold weather, and hunters could predictably locate and kill them. The way in which the aboriginal Indians in Florida killed manatees is not known, though it may have been similar to the methods used by the other native American groups.

The aboriginal Indian population in Florida probably numbered about 25,000 at the time the Europeans arrived there in about 1500. Two centuries later, the aboriginals were virtually eliminated, and members of several Indian tribes from the north (collectively called Seminoles) moved into the state. The Seminoles were hunters who took manatees for their meat, oil and bones. In fact, the Seminoles traded meat they did not use to white settlers. In 1896, Charles B. Cory provided a detailed description of the hunt:

> Many of these animals are killed by the Indians every year. They hunt them in canoes, sometimes in the river, and again in the ocean, but usually near the mouth of some river. These animals come to the surface every few minutes to breathe and their heads may be seen as they appear for a moment above the surface of the water.
>
> They harpoon them as they rise to the surface using a steel point barbed on one side, attached to the end of a long pole. To the steel point is fastened a strong cord, which in turn is attached to a float. Upon being struck the manatee sinks at once, but the direction in which he moves is indicated by the float. The Indians follow the float as closely as possible and watch for him to rise to the surface, when they shoot him through the head, and the huge animal is then towed to the shore. It requires considerable skill as well as strength to drive the harpoon through the thick, tough hide. Many of those animals grow to be very large size, and it is claimed that some of them have been taken which exceed twelve feet in length.

Although manatees were captured by Seminoles, the importance of the manatee in the Indian's diet is speculative. Peterson feels that the species was probably not a very significant resource for the Indians, at least by the end of the 19th century.

The level of take of manatees by white settlers is also uncertain. The settlers clearly took manatees for their meat (the tail, soaked in brine, was considered a particular delicacy), the fat and the hide, from which whips, oar locks and walking sticks were made. Typically, the manatees were shot or harpooned.

In the last quarter of the 19th century, a new demand and a new method of harvest came into being. Museums and aquaria sought manatees for their collections, and, of course, the specimen would be worthless with bullet or harpoon holes. Therefore, hunters used seine nets, stretched across likely waterways, to entangle and kill manatees. A cleaned skeleton and hide sold for US $100.

In the 20th century, hunting has continued, albeit at a slower pace. It probably continues today. In 1980, two butchered manatees were found in the Miami River in downtown Miami, and in 1985, a fisherman along Florida's east coast was convicted of killing a manatee for meat. Despite such events, it seems likely that deliberate harvest of manatees in Florida has nearly stopped, but other acts of human cruelty have been reported. Manatees have been shot with rifles or arrows by bored "sportsmen," they have been found with garden rakes embedded in their backs, and in one case, someone's initials had been carved into an animal's back. Fishermen have been observed deliberately snagging manatees with hooks, and people throw rocks at the large, slow-moving animals.

The question of the current status of the manatee in Florida, relative to its past status, has arisen repeatedly. Although a number of people have suggested that there were once thousands of manatees in Florida, that the population there nearly became extinct in the late 1800s and that today there exists a tiny remnant population, there is no strong evidence to support these points of views. Thomas J. O'Shea, leader of the Department of the Interior's Sirenia Project (U.S. Fish and Wildlife Service) in Gainesville, Florida, has critiqued historical and present data, and he suggests the following:

- Manatees in Florida are on the fringe of their range, occupying an area where cold winter weather prevented significant expansion of either the range or the size of the population;
- Due to hunting pressure by Indians and settlers, manatees were never extremely abundant in Florida;
- There is no compelling evidence that manatees approached extinction during the latter half of the 19th century;
- With reduced levels of hunting and poaching, as well as increased availability of warm water in winter and aquatic vegetation, manatee populations may actually have increased in the mid-1900s; and
- The Florida manatee's status is precarious today as a result of the impact of a rapidly rising human population.

The rapidly growing human population has increased the incidental manatee take. Manatees can drown if they become entangled in fishing nets and crab pot lines. Flood control dams and navigation locks can sometimes kill manatees as well. But the most frequent single cause of manatee mortality in Florida today involves collisions between manatees and watercraft.

The West Indian manatee has been subjected to regular harvest (either intentional or unintentional) for centuries, but there has been little commercial use of West Indian manatee products. The same is not true for the Amazonian manatee, found in the rivers of the Amazon basin in Brazil, Guyana, Colombia, Peru and Ecuador.

Certainly, native hunters have taken and used the products of Amazonian manatees for as long as records exist. Commonly, nets and harpoons were used to capture manatees, and then the animals were sometimes killed by plugging their nostrils with wooden pegs. The illegal take continues to this day at unknown levels, and the impact of subsistence harvest on the status of the species is unknown. Data exist, however, regarding commercial take of this species prior to its protection. Much of the following information comes from a thorough assessment done in 1982 by Daryl P. Domning.

In the 17th century, trade in Amazonian manatee meat was already a big business. In 1660, Father Antonio Viera noted that 20 Dutch ships were loaded annually with meat provided by the Nheengaiba Indians near Cabo Norte, Brazil. The meat in this case may have come from either Amazonian or West Indian manatees, because both could have been found in this area. However, meat clearly from Amazonian manatees was recorded to have been sold at Cayenne at this time for about three pence for about 0.5 kilograms (1 pound).

Records from the 18th century indicate a continuing high level of take. In two years in the mid-1780s, the Pesqueiro Real (Royal Fishery) da Villa Franca produced 3,873 *arrobas* (about 58,000 kilograms or 128,000 pounds) of dried and salted manatee meat and 1,613 *potes* (about 32,000–48,000

Two manatees rest just under the surface of the water, and, not far away, a motorboat races past. In Florida, collisions with watercraft kill more manatees than does any other human activity. Drawing by Marya Willis

kilograms or 70,000–106,000 pounds) of *manteiga* (lard). These products suggested a take over two years of about 1,500 manatees, which included all sizes and sexes, even pregnant females.

Records of Amazonian manatee catches for the early part of the 19th century are scarce, but many records from the mid-1800s until the 1930s are available and show some annual fluctuation. The primary commercial product during that period was *mixira*, fried manatee meat preserved in its own fat, but uncooked meat and lard were also sold. In some years, most of the *mixira* shipped from the interior was consumed in Manaus; other years, cities such as Belém received and consumed the bulk of the *mixira*. There are no indications that the *mixira* was exported beyond the Amazon area. Although it is impossible to calculate exactly how many manatees were killed to provide all the meat, *mixira* and lard recorded, Domning has concluded that the average annual take of Amazonian manatees for both commercial and subsistence uses in the 19th and early 20th centuries was several thousand.

This high level of take continued when the harvest focused on a new product, beginning in the 1930s, as commercial industry outside the Amazon sought manatee hides. Although manatee hide had been used traditionally for whips, shields, glue and, perhaps medicine, the difficulty encountered in tanning the hide kept demand relatively low. In 1934, a new process was developed, and manatee hides began to be used for machinery belts, gaskets, hoses and other durable products. Catch statistics suggest a take of 4,000 to 7,000 manatees a year between 1935 and 1954, when the industry collapsed, probably due to increased availablilty of synthetic substitutes for hides. Even though well over 100,000 manatees may have been taken in this 20-year period, there is no real indication that the manatee population in the Amazon had collapsed; however it is difficult to accurately assess the impact of the harvest on population size.

The final period of high commercial catch of Amazonian manatees came between 1954 and 1973, after which manatee hunting was prohibited. The product of choice this time was meat. Unlike the hide industry, which still permitted use of the meat by local people, the meat industry was superimposed on the subsistence take of manatees for meat. The peak recorded commercial take (which does not include catches for subsistence use) was 6,500 manatees in 1959. From that time until 1973, the harvest levels declined. Possibly, the decline indicates a significant reduction in the Amazonian manatee population.

The manatee population has also decreased in certain parts of the range of the West African manatee, along the Atlantic coast of Africa from Senegal to Angola, but the reductions do not reflect impacts of major commercial harvest. Rather, three factors seem to have led to redistribution or local extirpation of manatees in Africa: drought (which has caused reduction in available food and habitat for manatees), subsistence harvest and incidental or opportunistic take. James Powell, a zoologist who has worked with manatees in several West African countries, reports that a new problem has arisen when rivers have been dammed for hydroelectric or irrigation purposes. Apparently a large number of manatees died in Senegal several years ago when water levels in Lake Guire were lowered. West African manatees are also killed regularly in the gates of the dams.

Levels of subsistence harvest of West African manatees (which is illegal) are hard to quantify, but some general observations can be made. As indicated earlier, people in some parts of West Africa (such as Cameroon) often fear manatees and do not attempt to catch them; not all people share this point of view, however. Methods of hunting manatees in Africa vary somewhat from country to country, but a couple of examples illustrate the process.

In 1974, Sylvia Sykes, a zoologist in Nigeria, observed manatee harvesting by professional hunters of the Kabawa tribe, a semi-nomadic people who rely on fishing and manatee hunting. Prior to a manatee hunt, certain preparations must be made, as described by Sykes: "They build a platform of forked sticks bound together with bark rope on a submerged sand bar close to deep water. Long whippy rods are arranged about a foot apart in the deep water in front of the platform, to form a screen. A bunch of freshly plucked green grass, of a species favored by manatees, is tied loosely to the front of the platform, resting on the surface of the water."

The hunt itself begins at dusk, as the hunter seats himself on the platform. He is armed with a harpoon with a strong, sharp, detachable head possessing three or four barbs. A nylon line attaches the head to a palm float. As the hunter waits silently, he may notice two rods being forced apart, which indicates a manatee is attempting to reach the grass bait. At this time, the hunter rises silently, waits for the manatee to begin feeding, and then strikes hard. A successful strike leads him to shout "Praise God," the sign for his cohorts to chase the palm float in their canoes. When the float is retrieved, the men kill the manatee with a fishing spear. The next day, the carcass is illegally sold for local consumption or other uses for between £120 and £300.

Baited traps appear to be very commonly used by manatee hunters in West Africa, where chronic food shortages for manatees may make them vulnerable to being lured by food. For other sirenians a tendency to aggregate (when Amazonian manatees are subject to food shortages or during the dry season, or when Florida manatees gather at certain warm water discharges in winter) may make bait unnecessary. Except for the use by the Guiana Indians of the delectable moku-moku blossoms described earlier, the use of baits to catch sirenians outside West Africa appears rare.

James Powell has found two types of manatee hunters in Gambia: specialists at hunting manatees and opportunists who catch manatees while engaging in other activities. The specialist hunters catch manatees as their ancestors did, using a harpoon with a detachable head attached by a line to a float. These hunters also construct baited traps, much as the Kabawa do, if signs of manatees feeding are observed. The hunters seem to be declining in numbers, in part because many young men now elect to abandon hunting and work in a city for wages.

The specialist hunter is familiar with manatee behavior, as well as certain rituals for killing and butchering the animals. Other fishermen in Gambia know that knowledge of the proper rituals is important, and they are, thus, generally unwilling to engage in a deliberate hunt for manatees. However, these same fishermen appreciate the delicious meat of the manatee, and if one is found in their nets, the men happily divide the meat among the people of their village. Any meat left over is sold for as much as US $150, an extraordinary sum to these men.

The opportunistic hunters stretch a series of nets across a small stream or river called a bolon. The nets are used to entangle and trap many types of animals moving upstream or downstream. When a manatee encounters the nets, it generally becomes entangled and drowns. Manatees are also taken opportunistically if they are found in bolons as water recedes at the start of the dry season and the animals are killed by clubbing, harpooning or shooting. Finally, the opportunistic hunter sometimes builds brush barriers across a bolon; when a manatee approaches, but can not pass the barrier, it is shot or clubbed.

Other fishermen in Gambia, as well as in other West African countries, catch undetermined numbers of manatees strictly by accident. Placement of shark nets may be particularly damaging to manatees, with one report documenting five manatees killed in 87 days in a single location (Ngazobil, Senegal). Incidental take of other species of marine mammals has been shown to have a serious impact on wild populations, and it is possible that such is the case for certain local populations of manatees in Africa as well. Nonetheless, in most locations, the specialist hunter probably causes more damage than the opportunist.

According to Melissa Grigione, the Cameroon hunter Joseph, mentioned earlier, attended a school in Kongola State, Nigeria, for three years to learn to kill manatees, crocodiles, hippopotami and other animals. Apparently, the final examination is difficult, with only about 30% of the students passing; retests are permitted. A family runs the school, and most manatee hunters in Nigeria are members of the family. As part of the training, the head of the family presents students with charms to aid in hunting. In Joseph's case, the charm is a small box worn around the neck. Before Joseph kills a manatee, he prays with the Koran. He then spears the animal using the typical harpoon with a float attached.

Parts from manatees killed in Cameroon are used in an astounding number of ways. The meat, as usual, is delicious food. The dung may be used medicinally or, when rubbed on the body of a manatee hunter, to help effect a quick capture. The intestinal fat is rubbed on the body to relieve achy joints. The bones are used for medicine or as musical instruments and the ash from burned bones treats insect bites. Oil is used for cooking. And consumption of male manatee sex organs supposedly helps impotent male humans, a medical application for which the efficacy is in doubt!

With this great variety of subsistence uses, as well as the potential for profit from sale of the products, it is no surprise that manatees in West Africa have been wiped out of certain parts of their range (e.g., along the northern border of Benin) despite protective legislation. Although the manner by which manatees are taken in Africa, and the way in which the animals are used have been noted, it has been impossible to document the level of harvest or the effects of the harvest on the wild manatee populations of most areas.

Dugongs are harvested deliberately and incidentally in many parts of their range in the Indian and Pacific oceans. The incidental take of dugongs in particular parts of the world may occur most often in the course of shark, baramundi (a delicious fish) and turtle netting, as well as in nets designed to protect swimmers using beaches in Queensland, Australia, from shark attacks. In Sri Lanka and elsewhere, when dugongs are captured, the meat and other products are often sold in local markets.

The dugong, like the West African manatee, is also prey to subsistence hunting. Aboriginals in parts of Australia and Papua New Guinea, for example, are still permitted to take animals, as they have for thousands of years. In the islands in the Torres Strait, an isolated area between the Cape York peninsula (Queensland, Australia) and Papua New Guinea where both hunters and dugongs are relatively common, a traditional hunt may serve as a representative example. Although Torres Strait male islanders are all seamen, not all can claim to be real hunters. A real hunter is called a *buai garka*, which means "male family head," and he is the leader of the hunt. A *buai garka* must be extremely knowledgeable about the animals he hunts, the habitat they occupy and the best time and place to effect a catch. The *buai garka* is a highly respected individual, not only for his success in bringing dugong meat to his village, but also for surviving the dangers of the hunt. Dugong hunters can be caught in ropes and drown, they can dislocate shoulders as they strike their powerful prey, they can be knocked unconscious by a blow from a stricken dugong's tail, they can inadvertently step on a venomous stonefish, or they can be towed by a speared dugong far out to sea, where sudden storms can destroy their boats.

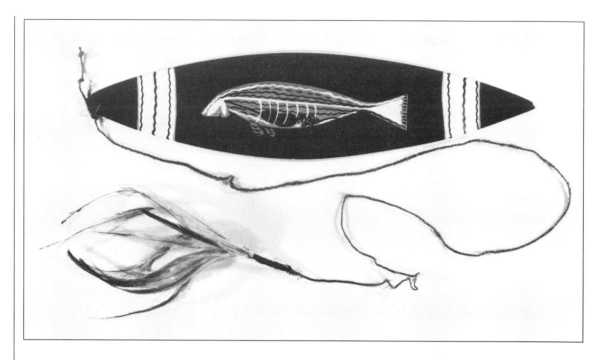

Despite the skill and knowledge of the *buai garka*, another factor is vital to the success of the hunt: luck. To ensure good luck, hunters have certain dos and don'ts that they must follow. For example, hunters may not hunt while they are in mourning after a relative dies; hunters may not hunt after a serious argument; they must not allow women or uninitiated men to touch hunting equipment; wives of crew members can not be pregnant; and hunters must avoid sexual intercourse the night before a hunt begins. In addition, individual hunters use special, personal charms and rituals to ensure that a dugong will approach the boat and be killed.

With all the rituals observed, hunters set out in their sail or motor-driven craft. Because hunting is often done at night or in water that is turbid, it can be difficult for hunters to see the dugongs underwater. Therefore, the men use clues such as uprooted seagrasses, bubbles, silt clouds, wakes and floating excrement to find the dugongs. Homing in on the secretive animals, the hunters attempt to find what they consider to be the best possible quarry—a fat, adult female dugong, called *ipaka dangal*. The islanders also have a name for a low-quality, thin dugong: *wati dangal*.

As the targeted dugong is approached, a harpooner stands in the bow of the boat, harpoon in hand. When the animal is positioned properly, the aboriginal leaps from the bow, plunging the harpoon through the dugong's tough skin and into the muscle beneath. The leap ensures that the full weight of the man is behind the blow, to be sure that the head of the harpoon is

The dugong plays an important role for many aboriginal tribes, and is represented in their carvings and paintings. This artifact, which makes a loud noise when it is spun around a person's head, was a gift to John Reynolds from Helene Marsh. It shows an outline of the digestive system of the dugong, an appropriate subject given his research on manatee digestive tract anatomy and hers on that of the dugong. Photograph by David Williams

secured. However, the leaping harpooner places himself in danger from the speared animal, as well as from the elements. In fact, as contact with the dugong is made, the hunter must immediately let go of the harpoon shaft and grab the boat as it is towed forward. The harpooned dugong is attached to the boat by a rope running from the head of the harpoon. But capture is not assured until crew members swim out to the animal and tie another rope around the tail. Once this is done, the crew haul the dugong to the side of the boat, and pull its tail out of the water, thereby holding the head underwater until the animal drowns.

The dead dugong is lashed to the side of the boat or manhandled into the craft. It is taken to the village, where it will be shared with the entire community. Since the capture of dugongs provides a major source of food and is often initiated by some special event (such as a birth, wedding, funeral or religious event), the villagers excitedly gather on the beach to observe the butchering, itself a ritualized affair. Researchers Bernard and Judith Nietschmann have described the butchering:

> Three or four of the men will butcher a dugong or turtle: the man who harpooned the animal, one of his mother's brothers, and one or two members of the hunting crew. Young boys help by washing pieces of meat in the sea. A complicated system is followed for butchering a dugong. Lines are scratched into the thick hide to act as guides for cutting. The number, names, and placement of these cutting lines have not changed since the first ethnographic descriptions were made in the late nineteenth century. There are at least forty-five names for different cuts of dugong meat.

Hunting tools include the Brazilian manatee harpoons (left), one of which was broken by a manatee that got away. Photograph by Daryl Domning
A wapo *(dugong harpoon), m ade of three nails bound together, is used to secure dugongs.* Photograph courtesy of Great Barrier Reef Marine Park Authority

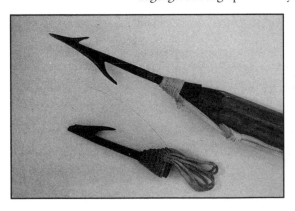 

The butchering provides a time for the villagers to socialize. The successful hunt reaffirms ties among villagers, as meat is freely shared by all. Later the villagers feast on the meat, and the hunt is relived.

The hunt described above is not typical of all coastal villages where dugong are available. In some villages, dugong hunting is prohibited. In others, only initiated older men can touch or eat dugong; if a woman, youth or child even touches water in which dugong grease floats, that person is said to become ill. Nor would there always be a village feast. Some hunters do not catch dugongs simply for subsistence use; rather they sell some animals they catch to local markets.

The combined subsistence and commercial use of dugongs in the Torres Strait means that the catch can be high. In the April 1984 issue of *Sirenews* (a newsletter edited by Daryl Domning), Helene Marsh, a leader in dugong research and management who is based at James Cook University of North Queensland in Australia indicated that the Torres Strait islanders estimated their 1983 catch of dugong to exceed 1,000 animals; official estimates, however, suggest that the 1983 take was more likely 400–500 dugong by the islanders. Depending on which life history parameters one assumes to be true of dugongs in the Torres Strait area, the minimum dugong population needed to sustain an annual kill of 400–500 dugongs should be between 9,000 and 29,000. The actual population size in that region was about 12,500 dugongs, Marsh noted in 1988.

The dugong population in the Torres Strait has declined considerably, due in part to overharvest by the islanders. This raises the question: Should the dugong harvest continue today? In a paper delivered in 1979, Athol Chase of Griffith University in Queensland, Australia, attempted to answer this question:

> Today, Aboriginals and Islanders are in a situation where there is great pressure to abandon old ways and to break continuity with the past in the raising of their children. Resettlement and relocation have brought attendant problems of ill-health, consumption of alcohol, loss of old skills and knowledge (even the use of indigenous languages), and a feeling of powerlessness which arises from operating in an over-institutionalized and foreign-dominated environment. There are people, however, who still attempt to make their traditions relevant to their own and their children's lives. The hunting and capture of dugongs in particular, is a major dimension of such attempts. To succeed in this activity is to gain a traditional status within the community. Indigenous cultures are, in some parts of Australia, in a critical state, often now dependent on the efforts of a handful of older men. To hunt from the sea is for a man of the sandbeach the proper and manly thing to do, and it gives evidence of one's skill and knowledge and an independence from the village store with its

introduced cash economy. While men go out hunting for dugongs, albeit in an aluminum boat with an outboard, there is some hope for the retention of indigenous cultural perspectives in a European dominated area. These, in addition to endangered species such as dugongs, have a right to survival.

Can dugongs in the Torres Strait survive continued high harvests by skilled hunters in modern motorboats? As discussed in greater detail in a later chapter, dugongs and the culture of the islanders may *both* survive if compromises can be reached, including a system of dugong sanctuaries, a strong education program in both Australia and Papua New Guinea, catch quotas, and, whenever possible, selective take of males and protection of pregnant females.

BENIGN USES OF SIRENIANS

Not all human interactions with sirenians are fatal. Two not-unrelated uses of manatees have been proposed, and in some places, implemented. Very large manatees ingest huge amounts of vegetation, perhaps up to 200 pounds per day. The first use simply employs manatees to eat lots of aquatic weeds to keep waterways open, the second to keep mosquito populations down by eliminating vegetation where the mosquitos spend part of their life cycle.

The ability of manatees to keep bodies of water clear of aquatic weeds was probably first noted at Georgetown, British Guiana (now called Guyana). In 1913, a dead manatee was found in a lake at the Botanic Gardens. The lake, which had been clear of vegetation, promptly became clogged with aquatic weeds. In a 1974 report, the National Science Research Council, Georgetown, Guyana, discussed the use of manatees as weed clearing agents in that country. Between 1954 and 1974, over 200 manatees were placed in weed-choked waterways, where they proved to be effective at keeping the weeds controlled. As an example, the report described an earth bottomed canal used as a water reservoir in 1951. Six weeks after it was built, the density of aquatic vegetation caused flow rate to drop to less than one meter per minute. Four men took 10 days to clear the canal, but two months later, the problem had returned. In 1952, four manatees were captured and placed in the canal; eight weeks later, the weeds were gone, and workers had to feed the hungry manatees with grass clippings from lawns. "During the 22 years the manatees have been in the canal there has been no weed problem." Many other examples demonstrate the effectiveness of manatees in Guyana's waterways.

Accounts such as this encourage use of manatees as weed-clearing agents. The animals did a spectacular job in Guyana, cost less than mechanical cropping or chemical control and do not pollute the environment with toxic chemicals. Further, they are harmless to people. A secondary proposed benefit was that the well-fed animals might multiply and be used as a readily available source of meat. In fact, the manatees that were effective in clearing weeds were apparently not well-fed, but half-starved, and manatees in canals were regularly poached. For these reasons, as well as their low reproductive potential, animals used in weed clearance have not formed a commercial breeding stock.

Many countries have expressed an interest in stocking weed-clogged waterways with hungry manatees. Experiments have been staged in Mexico and in the United States, and agencies have expressed interest in Pakistan, the United Arab Republic and Kariba Lake in Rhodesia. Although the status of most of the various projects or proposals could not be determined, the results of a Florida experiment are well known.

A 1966 report from Florida Atlantic University stated that since 1949, hundreds of millions of dollars were invested into a network of canals stretching over 1,100 miles (1,800 kilometers) in the state of Florida. The purposes of this huge project were flood control and water conservation. In 1966, it was estimated that costs of weed control when the system was completed would exceed $500,000 per year using conventional methods. Therefore, as an experiment, manatees were introduced into a canal to demonstrate their weed-clearing ability and to give scientists a good chance for observation of the animals. Eight manatees were captured between May 1964 and July 1965. The manatees showed excellent ability to keep small canals free of aquatic weeds, but by February 1966, seven of the eight had died: one had been shot and stabbed by vandals, four died from respiratory infections following cold weather (the animals lacked any warm water refuge), one died from "digestive failure," and one died from undetermined causes. Although project managers wanted to continue to work with manatees, the experiment ended in 1966.

In Florida, where periodic cold can kill or debilitate manatees that lack access to warm water refuges, year-round use of the manatees in canals that lack such access is dangerous. In addition, given the small manatee population in Florida, as well as the tremendous number of canals, lakes and other waterways that are clogged with weeds there today, manatees are probably not the solution. As a matter of fact, Kay Etheridge and her coworkers estimated that in one location (Kings Bay, Crystal River, Florida), it would take 1,050 manatees (almost the entire estimated manatee population of the state) 120 days to consume the standing biomass of hydrilla; this estimate does not even take into account plant productivity, which would replace standing biomass.

Manatees were used to control mosquitos in a seven-acre lagoon off the Chagres River in the Republic of Panama between 1963 and 1965. In this area, two types of mosquitoes take advantage of the dense aquatic vegetation to proliferate. *Mansonia* mosquitos have underwater pupal and larval stages in which the immature insects attach their breathing tubes to the aerated roots of certain plants. Populations of *Anopheles* (mosquitos that are malaria vectors) were supported by the dense vegetation, which reduced predation by small fishes. The job of the manatees was to reduce the favorable habitat for the mosquitoes.

Ten manatees (nine West Indian and one Amazonian) were captured and placed in the lagoon. Five animals escaped. The remaining five were observed for two years. Although the sirenians lived up to their reputation as big eaters, the project was not a success, primarily because, in the tropical climate of Panama, the vegetation grew faster than five manatees could eat it. It was estimated that 1,000–2,000 manatees would be needed to keep plant growth in the seven-acre lagoon under control. Although the experiments with manatees show that, if manatees were abundant enough, and if they were maintained in an appropriately controlled environment, they could be useful as natural weed-clearing agents, in reality, such use is generally not feasible.

HUMANS CAN HELP MANATEES, TOO

At least two human activities in Florida, canal building and power production, have inadvertently helped manatees. There are hundreds of miles of canals in Florida, many choked with aquatic weeds, including exotic plants such as water hyacinth and hydrilla. To the manatees, dense weeds represent a major food source, as well as a sanctuary from motor boats, which kill and maim manatees. At one of the state's major natural warm springs at Crystal River, manatees can remain warm in winter, yet also be nourished from the luxuriant hydrilla that grows there. In addition, manatees at Crystal River are protected from people. As a consequence of the protection and food availability, the number of manatees using Crystal River as a winter refuge has risen steadily from 63 manatees in 1967-68 to nearly 300 in 1990.

Artificial warm-water refuges also exist in Florida. The majority of these are at power plants located in Tampa Bay, along the Caloosahatchee River in Fort Myers, at Fort Lauderdale, Riviera Beach, Fort Pierce and near Cape Canaveral. During normal operation, the plants discharge warm water as a by-product of electrical power generation. (Small numbers of manatees also seek refuge from cold at a group of industrial outfalls in the Jacksonville area and a paper plant near St. Mary's, Georgia.) Four plants operated by Florida Power & Light Company have each been observed to shelter over 200 manatees: the Cape Canaveral plant, Riviera plant, Port Everglades plant (in Fort Lauderdale) and the Fort Myers plant. The largest aggregation of manatees on record occurred on January 19, 1985, at Fort Myers: 338 animals in one survey. The power plants clearly provide sanctuary from cold for a

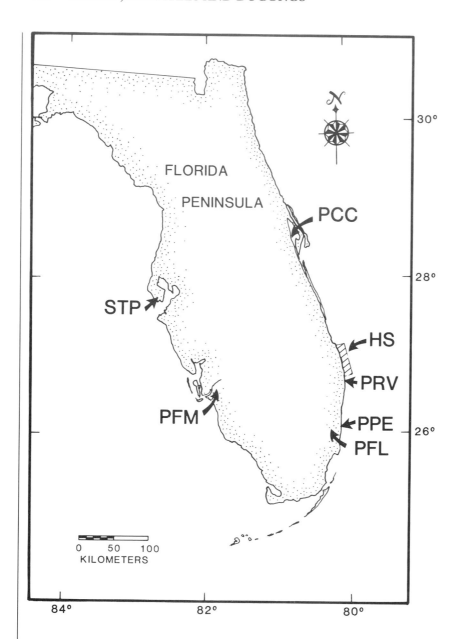

Power plants in Florida serve as important warm-water refuges for manatees. The record count for one location is 338 manatees at the Ft. Myers plant. Asterisks indicate plants where over 200 manatees have been observed at one time.

* PCC: *Cape Canaveral plant in Titusville*   PFL: *Lauderdal plant*
  HS: *Hobe Sound feeding area*   * PFM: *Ft. Myers plant*
* PRV: *Riviera Plant*   STP: *St. Petersburg*
* PPE: *Port Everglades plant in Ft. Lauderdale*

Drawing by David Williams

significant portion of the manatee population in the southeastern United States.

However, the power plant may, under certain circumstances, be a mixed benefit. Consider what would happen if a plant were to shut down unexpectedly during cold weather; the manatees seeking refuge there would literally "be out in the cold." This is exactly what happened in 1977, when a partial shut-down of a plant was implicated in the deaths due to cold-related illness of 38 manatees in Brevard and nearby counties in Florida's east coast. Or, manatees might seek refuge at a plant in the northern part of the range, rather than migrating to southern Florida. Truly exceptional cold weather (as occurred in December 1989) could lower water temperatures to the point where the warmth provided by the plant was insufficient; this may have contributed to the cold-related mortality of nearly 50 manatees in winter 1989–90. Consider also what would happen if a plant that had traditionally been a major source of warmth for manatees was retired; animals that had learned to come to the plant for refuge might remain there, awaiting warm water, and thus not reach shelter when cold weather arrived.

These dangerous possibilities have led management of power companies to be sure that they keep warm water flowing if at all possible when manatees seek refuge at the plants and plan ahead for the retirement of plants so that alternate sources of warm water can be provided. Florida Power & Light Company has not only been an industrial leader in funding manatee research and education efforts, but it has also provided an alternative source of warm water at the Fort Myers plant. When manatees are present, but the plant is not operating, a pump brings 27° C (81° F) water from a specially dug deep well to the surface, where it bathes the cold animals.

Interactions between humans and sirenians have generally been detrimental to the animals. Yet so far, only the Steller's sea cow and a few local populations of sirenians have succumbed to this sort of pressure. As the 20th century ends, however, the impact of direct interaction may become negligible, compared with the broader consequences of widespread habitat destruction.

THE
FLORIDA
MANATEE

Most Floridians have heard of manatees, but relatively few people encounter this massive, yet secretive creature in the wild. Indeed, unless someone deliberately seeks out manatees at one of the locations where they are known to gather in the winter, there is little likelihood that a manatee will be encountered. And those encounters can be traumatic: a wading fisherman may hear a sudden, loud breath then turn to see a grayish creature six times his size surface beside him. The monster may even nuzzle the person's legs before moving silently out of sight.

Although many people know "something" about Florida manatees, much of what the public knows might surprise the scientists who study this fascinating marine mammal. Daryl Domning once wrote that people should "never underestimate a sirenian," and Domning's scientific colleagues would agree. Though manatees are rare and are affected by a variety of human activities, they show an adaptability and a toughness that suggest that, given half a chance, Florida manatees may survive better than many people might expect.

RANGE

All living sirenians are found in warm tropical and subtropical waters. The Florida manatee may be found as far north as Virginia and as far west as Mississippi or Louisiana during warm summer months. Its year-round range is restricted to peninsular Florida and possibly southern Georgia and scientists consider animals outside these states to be extralimital wanderers. Florida manatees have also been found in Bahamian waters on rare occasions. Manatees may be found in any waterway that is over 1 meter (3.28 feet) deep and connected with coastal waterways, and the Florida manatee inhabits bays, estuaries, rivers and coastal areas where seagrasses and other vegetation abound. Manatees rarely venture into deeper, ocean waters, although there are reports of manatees in locations as far offshore as the Dry Tortugas Islands. Manatees live in both freshwater and saltwater and move readily between the two extremes. They can live indefinitely in freshwater, but we do not know how long they can survive in saltwater.

The primary range of the manatee along the Atlantic coast of Florida extends from the St. Johns River in northeastern Florida southward to the Miami area. The Indian River lagoon is a very important feeding area. Few manatees occur in the Florida Keys or in Florida Bay, and this area is somewhat of a gap (but not a barrier) in manatee distribution between the Atlantic and Gulf coasts. On the Gulf coast of Florida, manatees are abundant in the waters of the Everglades National Park, and their range extends northward to the Suwannee River in summer and sporadically westward.

LEGEND
⊠ YEAR ROUND
⊠ SEASONAL OR OCCASIONAL

Range of the Florida manatee. Cross-hatched areas may be occupied by manatees year-round. During warm months, manatees may travel as far north as Chesapeake Bay and as far west as Mississippi and Louisiana. Drawing by Leslie Ward

Manatees can be killed by freezes and cold snaps, and in winter the population shifts southward to warmer waters. Crystal River, in Citrus County, Florida, is the northern limit of the manatees' winter range on the Gulf Coast. Manatees congregate at the natural warm water springs there and at Blue Spring State Park, on the St. Johns River, near the east coast of Florida. On the Atlantic coast, the manatees' winter range historically was probably south of the Sebastian River. However, more recently, manatees have used warm water discharged from power plants as a source of warmth during cold winter weather. Among the most important of the artificial warm water discharges are Florida Power & Light Company's plants at Cape Canaveral, Fort Lauderdale, Port Everglades, Riviera and Fort Myers, and Tampa Electric Company's Apollo Beach plant in Tampa Bay. These artificially heated sources have conditioned manatees to expect warm water, so that many manatees now remain north of their historic wintering grounds. At each of four plants (Cape Canaveral, Riviera, Port Everglades and Fort Myers), more than 200 manatees have been counted in single aerial surveys during very cold weather.

ANATOMY

The Florida manatee (*Trichechus manatus latirostris*) is a distinct subspecies of the West Indian manatee (*Trichechus manatus*). Its subspecific status was originally proposed in 1934, but little anatomical evidence for the distinction was established. Due to lack of information, the Florida manatee and the Antillean manatee (*Trichechus manatus manatus*) were later considered by most writers a single species without subspecific division. It was not until the 1980s that sufficient anatomical material was available to allow scientists to confirm the subspecific distinction on the basis of skull characteristics.

The Florida manatee has a spindle-shaped body that is elliptical in cross section. It may reach a length of 3.9 meters (about 13 feet) and a weight of 1,500 kilograms (3,500 pounds). The average adult manatee is about 3 meters (10 feet) long and weighs about 500 kilograms (1,200 pounds). The tail is rounded and paddle-shaped. Hind limbs are absent but vestigial pelvic bones

A Florida manatee. The facial hairs, or vibrissae, may help it respond to its surroundings. Drawing by Leslie Ward

are found deep in the pelvic musculature. The front limbs are short (compared to those of most terrestrial mammals), very flexible and have three to four fingernails.

The skin is generally gray to brown in color and hairs are scattered over the body. Apparent skin color often depends on organisms, such as algae, found growing on it. The skin texture is rough. The eyes are small and located on the sides of the head. Manatees lack an external ear and the ear opening is very tiny and difficult to find. Whiskers (vibrissae) are prominent on the manatee's large, flexible upper lip. The lips themselves are used along with the flippers in manipulating vegetation when the manatee is feeding.

The life span of the manatee is not known with certainty. One captive manatee at the Bradenton Museum in Florida is over 40 years old. Age determination studies in dugongs using growth layers in their tusks indicate that they can live to be 60–70 years old, and it is reasonable to expect that manatees can do the same. In 1990, studies conducted by Miriam Marmontel at the University of Florida indicated that parts of the manatee's periotic (ear) bones have growth layers that may persist for the life of the animal and can be used for age estimation. Longevity over 50 years has been suggested using this technique.

The internal anatomy of the manatee generally has been known for over a hundred years, but for many organs and organ systems modern histological and histochemical techniques need to be applied to understand their function. The skeleton has been well described. The genus *Trichechus* is unique in that

Skull of the Florida manatee, Trichechus manatus latirostris. Drawing by Leslie Ward

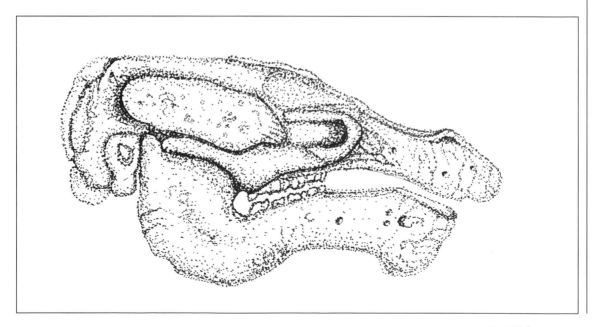

the manatees have only six cervical vertebrae compared with the seven of most other mammals. (The two-toed sloth is the only other mammal that normally has six cervical vertebrae.) Manatee bones are extremely dense and most lack marrow cavities. These dense pachyostotic (swollen) bones have been considered by some to be a result of the manatee's low metabolic rate or the result of "retarded" development. However, they may have a very important function as ballast to offset the positive buoyancy due to the large lungs and the intestinal gas generated by microorganisms in the process of digesting plant cellulose. Marrow (one site of red blood cell production) is found within the vertebrae and the sternum (breast bone). Red blood cells may also be produced by the liver.

THE SENSES

The sensory systems of the manatee have not been well studied. This is becoming an increasingly important area of investigation as scientists try to learn how manatees can avoid water vessels.

Anatomically, manatees have extremely large ear bones and may have a good sense of hearing. These bones are already well developed in newborn manatees. Observations in the field indicate that vocalizations play a key role in keeping the mother and calf together. A number of scientists have described the "duet" between a female and her calf, where the two animals alternate chirping to one another. In an incident in the Miami River in the 1970s, a

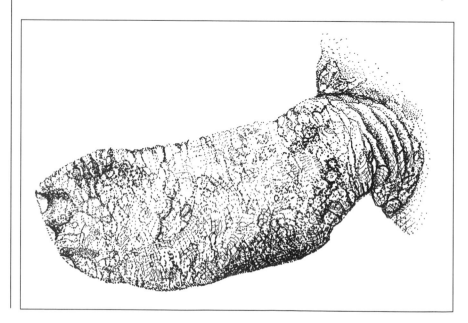

The flipper of a West Indian manatee. Note the nails, which are lacking in Amazonian manatees. Drawing by Leslie Ward

A female manatee and her calf. Vocalizations play a role in keeping mother and calf together. Drawing by Marya Willis

female and her young calf were trapped behind an earthen dam separating a water-filled quarry from the river. Staff from the Miami Seaquarium were able to capture the calf but not the mother and had to release the calf back into the quarry at the end of the day. Although the water was extremely turbid, the mother came directly to the calf as soon as it was placed in the water, probably homing in on sounds made by the calf. The next day, the calf was recaptured but held as a lure for the mother in shallow water; sure enough, the mother approached and was also captured. Both animals were released unharmed on the other side of the dam. Fishermen in South America have used similar strategies to capture manatees.

Manatee sounds can be described as chirps, whistles or squeaks, have peak energies in the 3–5 kilohertz (or thousands of cycles/second) range, and are probably produced in the larynx, the region where humans and most other mammals produce sounds. It has been suggested but not confirmed that the

most sensitive location on the manatee's head for sound reception is not the tiny ear openings located several centimeters behind the eyes, but the area near the cheek bones, which are large and seem to be quite oily compared with other bones in the skull, and which are in direct contact with the ear bones. This arrangement is similar to that of dolphins, in which it is theorized that sound enters the fat-filled lower jaw and is conducted to the bullae (ear bones), apparently bypassing the tiny ear canal.

In addition, anatomical studies suggest that manatees are adapted to hear infrasound, frequencies too low to be heard by the human ear (generally less than 20 hertz). Physiological studies using contact hydrophones and small electrodes have also demonstrated the manatee's sensitivity to low frequencies. Recent studies on elephants (the distant relatives of the manatee) have shown that estrous females attract male elephants by producing very low frequency sounds. These sounds can actually attract male elephants when recordings are played with no female elephants in sight. Such sounds travel great distances in air, and could travel even further underwater. Manatee biologists have often

Socializing manatees may be observed nuzzling one another. Drawing by Marya Willis wondered how several male manatees managed to find an estrous female all at the same time. Infrasound produced by the female may be the answer.

Manatees have small (about 2 centimeters or .8 inches in diameter) but well-developed eyes. Their visual capabilities in clear water have not been well studied, but manatees seem to be able to detect objects from distances of tens of meters. The retina has both rods and cones, which suggests that manatees can see in both dim and bright light, and, perhaps, see color.

Manatees have taste buds at the back of their tongues, and reduced turbinate (internal nasal) bones on which olfactory tissue is presumably located. While the manatee can undoubtedly taste and is probably able to smell, its chemoreceptive capabilities have not been well studied. John Bengtson studied manatee food preferences at Blue Spring off the lower St. Johns River. He presented manatees with a variety of natural foods and found that although they would eat just about anything, they seemed to avoid a few species of plants known to contain noxious natural compounds. Besides using chemoreception to avoid ingesting certain plants, manatees may use taste and/or smell to recognize other individuals and to determine whether a female is in estrous.

Touch is a sense that appears to be important for manatees. Females and calves maintain lots of body contact. Manatees in general seem to like body contact with each other, as well as with a variety of inanimate objects. Some manatees at Crystal River seek out physical contact with divers while others actively avoid the divers. The 3- to 5-centimeter-long (1- to 2-inch-long) hairs scattered over the surface of their bodies may be used to detect the touch of other animals or water movements created by movement of nearby manatees.

FOOD AND WATER

The Florida manatee is, like the other sirenians, a herbivore. It feeds on a wide variety of submerged, emergent, floating and shoreline vegetation. In saltwater, manatees feed primarily on several species of seagrasses, including turtle grass (*Thalassia testudinum*), manatee grass (*Syringodium filiforme*) and shoal grass (*Halodule wrightii*). They may also eat some species of algae, mangrove leaves and red mangrove seedlings. In freshwater, they feed on a wide variety of plants, including *Hydrilla verticillata*, algae and water hyacinth (*Eichhornia crassipes*). These opportunistic feeders have even been known to crop overhanging branches, consume acorns, and haul themselves partially out of the water to consume bank vegetation. Manatees in Florida have been known to feed on over 60 species of plants, but they do avoid certain plants, such as some blue-green algae, that contain natural toxins.

The Florida manatee is flexible in its feeding habits in that it is able to feed on the bottom, in the middle of the water column, at the surface and on overhanging and bank vegetation. (This is in contrast with the dugong, which is strictly a bottom feeder.) The flippers and the upper lips of Florida manatees are used to manipulate or hold large pieces or clumps of plant material. The left and right lips can operate somewhat independently as they maneuver food into the mouth. Manatees lack front teeth but have thick, ridged pads at the front of the upper and lower jaws. These pads help break the vegetation into smaller pieces that are further chewed by the manatees' grinding molars.

Manatees have six to eight molars in each of their four (two upper and two lower) rows of teeth. These teeth are almost unique in that they are continually being replaced in a horizontal (back to front) manner throughout the life of the manatee. This unusual situation contrasts with that in the average terrestrial mammal, in which tooth replacement is vertical and discontinuous.

Using its flexible lips to help pull vegetation into its mouth, a manatee consumes huge amounts of vegetation daily. Drawing by Marya Willis

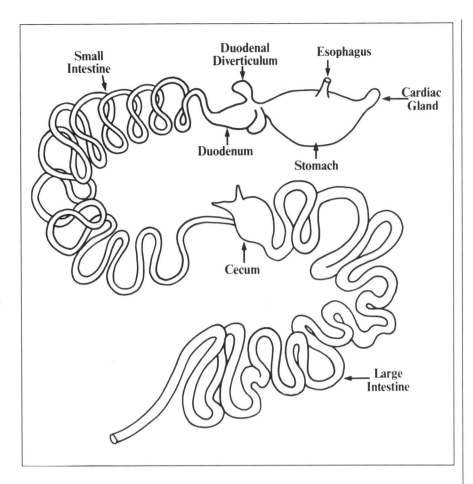

The lengthy digestive tract of the manatee is typical of most herbivores. Drawing by Daniel K. Odell, based on figure by Douglas Burn

The process of horizontal tooth replacement is shared with one species of kangaroo. The horizontal forces generated when the teeth come together (occlude) during chewing push the tooth row forward. This process continually provides new chewing surfaces as the teeth wear down.

Tooth movement in calves begins when their diet switches from milk to vegetation. A consequence of manatee tooth replacement is that scientists cannot use teeth to age individuals, as is commonly done in many other species of mammals.

As with most herbivorous mammals, the process of digestion begins with chewing to break up the food particles. Manatees also have large salivary glands that produce saliva, which lubricates food as it passes into the esophagus and assists with digestion. The manatee has a rather large digestive tract, as is typical of a herbivore. The esophagus ends in a large, muscular, single-compartment stomach with a large digestive (cardiac) gland on one side. The gland produces huge amounts of mucus, hydrochloric acid and the enzyme pepsin. The stomach empties into an enlarged duodenum (upper small intestine) of nearly equal volume. For some time, until proper histological studies were done, it was thought that the duodenum was a second stomach compartment. The duodenum has two tiny horn-shaped diverticula (blind sacs) at its junction with the stomach. The duodenum empties into the small intestine, which may be as long as 20 meters (about 65 feet) in a large manatee. Despite its length, the small intestine is narrow. At the junction of the small and large intestines is a large, two-horned cecum, corresponding to the human appendix. The large intestine may be as long as the small intestine, but its diameter is several times greater.

At the cecum and in the large intestine, the bulk of the digestive processes occur. Food particle size is rapidly reduced with the help of microorganisms, including anaerobic bacteria, that break down the plant material (cellulose) by fermentation. The end products of this breakdown process (called cellulolysis) are a variety of volatile fatty acids that are absorbed in the intestine. Another product of digestion in manatees is methane gas (expulsion of which often provides an easy way to locate submerged manatees). Food takes about seven days to pass through the manatee's digestive tract.

The digestive process in manatees typifies the so-called hindgut digesters, herbivores in which most cellulose breakdown occurs in the large intestine. The horse is another hindgut digester. Ruminants, such as cows and sheep, are also herbivores, but they digest most of the cellulose in their food using microorganisms located in the expanded stomach compartments, and, hence, are called foregut digesters.

A source of freshwater is also important. Most marine mammals (whales, dolphins, porpoises, seals, sea lions, etc.) seem to obtain the required amounts of freshwater from the food that they eat or from metabolism of fat reserves or, like the sea otter, they have efficient kidneys and can extract freshwater from sea water.

The Amazonian manatee lives in freshwater and, therefore, does not have a problem obtaining water to drink. The West Indian and West African manatees live in both freshwater and saltwater and may require a source of freshwater for drinking. Florida manatees are often seen drinking from hoses and other freshwater sources and congregating at river mouths, but it is not known whether they can live in saltwater indefinitely. Certainly, manatees can occupy marine habitats for rather long periods, as demonstrated by both the presence of large barnacles growing on manatees' skin and the sighting of manatees in remote areas such as the Dry Tortugas, where freshwater is not available. Scientists have taken advantage of manatees' need or desire for freshwater to capture and tag the manatees with radio and satellite transmitters. The animals are attracted to a particular area by a freshwater hose; while they drink intently, the scientists quietly stretch a net behind them.

The manatee kidney is a flattened, lobulated organ (similar to a cow's kidney, but very different from the reniculate kidney of whales and seals) and has a structure that suggests that a reasonably concentrated urine can be produced. Kidney function has not been studied, but preliminary investigations have shown that manatees in saltwater produce a more concentrated urine than manatees in freshwater.

Most scientists believe that Florida manatees can exist for some time without freshwater, but that the animals must have access to freshwater periodically to survive. Therefore, it is important that adequate freshwater sources be a component of manatee conservation strategies.

BREATHING AND DIVING

Manatees, like other marine mammals, do most of their feeding underwater and must be able to hold their breath long enough to feed efficiently. Marine mammals have a number of adaptations that allow them to stay under water longer than the average terrestrial mammal. While at rest, a large manatee can stay submerged for 20 minutes. Smaller manatees and active manatees breathe more frequently. The average interval between breaths is two to three minutes. Early studies by the well-known physiologists P.F. Scholander and Laurence Irving showed that manatees strapped to a board and forcibly submerged exhibited the typical rapid decrease in heart rate (bradycardia) seen in other diving animals. We assume that under voluntary diving conditions the manatee's heart rate would still decrease but less dramatically. However, free diving and diving metabolism have not yet been studied extensively in the Florida manatee. Voluntary-diving studies using captive Amazonian manatees indicate that their heart rate does not decrease during routine dives, but that it does decrease (from about 40 beats per minute to about 8) when they are frightened.

Manatees breathe through two valved nostrils situated at the tip of the head. Manatees exhale on surfacing and studies by Michael Bergey indicate that, like cetaceans, manatees can renew about 90% of the air in their lungs in a single breath. (Humans at rest generally renew about 10% of the air in the lungs in a single breath.) The lungs are flattened and may be 1 meter (about 3 feet) long. The major bronchi (large-diameter airways) extend the full length of the lung. The lungs are situated above the horizontally placed hemidiaphragms (two half-width diaphragms), another unusual anatomical feature of the sirenians, in which each lung is in a separate cavity with a separate diaphragm. The hemidiaphragms extend laterally from the centra (bodies) of the vertebrae to the body wall. We do not know whether the pleural cavities

can function independently but we do know that manatees can have severe infections in one lung even though the other seems to function normally.

The shape and placement of the lungs makes sense when one considers the horizontal position with which manatees float in the water. Changing the volume of the lungs, perhaps by contracting or relaxing the diaphragm, apparently allows the manatee to hang motionless in the water column and to move up or down with little apparent effort. As mentioned above, the manatee's heavy skeleton may also play a role in buoyancy control. Good buoyancy control is important when the manatee is feeding on the bottom. By not having to exert itself to stay on the bottom, the manatee can stay down longer and feed more efficiently.

A manatee comes to the surface to breathe. Manatees can remain underwater for as long as 20 minutes. Drawing by Marya Willis

TEMPERATURE REGULATION AND MIGRATION

Observations of animals at the climatic extremes of their ranges often give insight into aspects of the animals' biology that are not immediately apparent in the center of the range, where the climate may be more stable. Florida manatees are sensitive to water temperature and move into warm-water sites when water temperature drops below about 20° C (68° F). We know that severe cold weather (temperatures at or near freezing for several days) kills manatees in Florida. The juveniles appear to be particularly sensitive. Preliminary work by Blair Irvine (formerly with the U.S. Fish and Wildlife Service in Florida) suggests that the manatee's fat layer may be an ineffective insulator and that the manatee has only limited abilities to increase its metabolic rate to compensate for heat loss during cold weather. In addition, the manatee's resting (basal) metabolic rate is only 15%-22% of that predicted for a terrestrial mammal of similar body weight. Cold weather may cause manatees to stop feeding. Manatees found dead after periods of cold weather have often depleted their body cavity fat, stopped feeding (no food in stomach), and are dehydrated. Juveniles may be more sensitive to cold than larger animals because of a critical body size with respect to the potential for heat loss (body surface area to body mass ratio). Younger calves may not suffer because they get plenty of energy from their mother's milk. In Florida, unpredictably cold winter weather is a major natural manatee mortality factor that must be considered in management plans. High human-caused mortality coupled with unpredictably high natural mortality (as occurred in late 1989) could be disastrous to the population, particularly if recruitment (addition of new individuals to the population) rate is low.

To escape the colder water and air temperatures, manatees migrate to and from natural and artificial warm water refuges following the passing of periodic cold fronts. These movements can be documented using aerial and ground-based surveys and by tracking movements of individual animals with radio and satellite telemetry. While the population in general shifts to the south in winter, many animals make shorter north-south (and vice-versa) movements in between cold fronts. For example, many manatees that summer in northeastern Florida spend at least part of the winter basking in warm water at the Riviera and Port Everglades power plants. During warm spells between cold fronts, the manatees may leave the areas of the plants to feed. A common feeding area is located at Hobe Sound, thirty kilometers north of the Riviera plant.

The development and application of radio and satellite telemetry by the U.S. Fish and Wildlife Service has opened a new window through which we can view manatees. Electronic links, especially through satellites, now allow us to see where a tagged manatee goes both day and night, how fast it moves and what its preferred habitats are. Individual manatees have been tracked from Georgia to Miami. Identification of preferred habitat is extremely important for managing human activities that have an impact on manatees (coastal development, navigation channels, boat speeds, dredging); only by identifying critical habitat needs of manatees can those resources be protected.

REPRODUCTION

The age-specific aspects of manatee reproduction are not thoroughly known because a method of age determination has only recently been described. However, based on field observations of recognizable individuals, it appears that manatees may become sexually mature at 6–10 years of age (some younger and probably some older), at a body length of about 2.7 meters (about 8.5 feet). In males the testes weight increases dramatically when animals attain this size. Some spermatogenesis has been found in male manatees as small as 2.37 meters (7.8 feet). Although it is thought that adult female manatees may grow somewhat longer and bulkier than males, it is generally impossible to tell the sex of an individual animal unless its underside can be observed. Both sexes have an umbilical scar approximately midway along the belly. In males, the genital opening lies further toward the tail from the umbilicus, and the anus lies some distance further caudal. In females, the genital opening exists near the anus, with both openings located closer to the tail.

Of course there are other ways to confirm that a manatee is a female. The presence of a suckling calf, extremely rotund appearance during pregnancy, and swelling of the genital area during estrous would all identify a female animal.

Mating can take place either at the surface or underwater. Often, more than one male mates with an estrous female, and no single posture is assumed during copulation. Some pairs remain horizontal in the water column, others vertical. Frequently, the bull turns upside down and swims below the female, but mating can also take place with the animals on their sides, facing one another.

Based on reproduction of captive manatees and some recent field observations, the gestation period is at least 12 months. (Some scientists believe that the gestation period is closer to 13 months.) Most births are of a single calf about 120 centimeters (about 47 inches) long and weighing 30 kilograms (66 pounds). A few cases of twins have been documented. The details of the birth process remain unclear but observations of calving in captive manatees have shown that the offspring can be born either head- or tail-first.

In the field, females usually seek quiet areas in which to give birth. In Florida, newborn calves can be seen at any time of year, although more seem to be born in spring and summer.

In the few cases in which births have been observed in captivity, the newborn calf is capable of swimming to the surface on its own, although the attentive behavior of the mother may give the impression that she is assisting the calf. Calves vocalize at or soon after birth and this is probably an important part of the mother-calf bonding process. The calf begins to nurse within a few hours after birth, and nursing frequency and duration increases as the calf becomes more proficient. Unlike many mammals, the mammary glands are located in an axillary (armpit) position, somewhat similar to their pectoral position in humans.

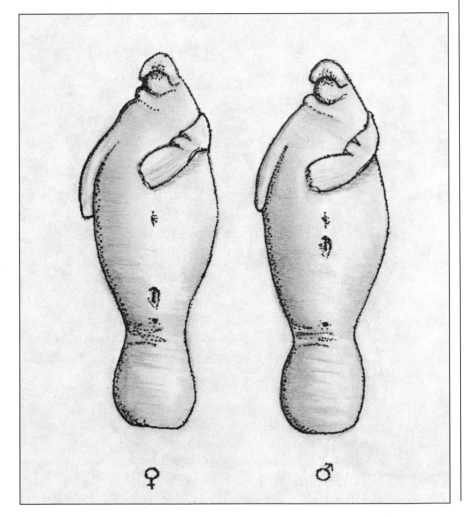

By observing the ventral (belly) side of a sirenian, one can easily tell what sex the animal is. Females (left) have an umbilical scar located some distance anterior to the genital and anal openings. In males (right), the genital opening is located very close to the umbilical scar, and the anus is located by itself, in a posterior position. Drawing by Leslie Ward

A calf may stay with its mother for one to two years, even though it is probably nutritionally independent by the end of its first year. It must learn the locations of feeding areas, warm-water refuges and migratory routes from its mother.

The calving interval is on the order of two to five years, but a female who loses a calf is able to resume estrous cycling and have another calf in a little over a year. Mature females seem to have an estrous cycle that approximates a lunar month. They are apparently polyestrous (more than one estrous cycle per year) and will continue cycling until they become pregnant.

A nursing manatee calf attaches itself to a nipple located in the "armpit," or axillary region of the mother. Drawing by Marya Willis

MANATEE BEHAVIOR

Manatee behavior has been studied for a relatively long period in Florida. Significant contributions were made in the 1950s by Joseph Curtis Moore, who documented manatees congregating at the power plant effluent in the

Miami River and provided general notes on the distribution and natural history of the manatee in Florida. Moore's unpublished field notes contain one of the original manatee propeller-scar catalogs that he used to identify individual animals. He also documented mating herds.

In the late 1960s, Daniel Hartman began a long-term study of manatee behavior at Crystal River, Florida. Hartman's doctoral dissertation, together with other data he collected, became a special publication of the American Society of Mammalogists, and remains the premier reference available on details of manatee behavior. He too used propeller scars to identify individual animals. This study continues today under the supervision of the U.S. Fish and Wildlife Service.

Manatees have been described as semisocial. With the exception of winter congregations at warm-water refuges, the basic social unit of the Florida manatee is the female and her calf. Other groupings appear to be transient. As stated above, the calf is dependent on its mother not only for nutrition, but also for information on feeding and resting areas, travel routes and warm-water refuges.

The precocious calves are able to swim with their mothers within minutes of birth. A young animal commonly remains close to its mother's side. Adult manatees typically swim in single file, but a calf always travels parallel to its mother, directly behind her flipper. It is possible that the animals can communicate most effectively in this position, or the formation is hydrodynamically advantageous if the calf experiences less drag from the water.

The females do not attack other manatees or humans that approach their young. Instead, they attempt to keep other manatees and human divers away from their calves by swimming between the intruder and their offspring. If the danger is perceived as severe, the female and the calf will flee. A fleeing female—calf pair produce a duet, with one animal vocalizing and the other emitting an answering call. In one instance near Blue Lagoon, a female manatee was separated from her young by a partly opened floodgate. The opening was too small for the mother to pass, and the current was too strong for the calf to swim back upstream through the opening. For at least three hours, the mother manatee attempted to maintain contact with her calf by repeatedly placing her head through the narrow opening of the gate and vocalizing. Eventually, the gate opened enough so that she could swim through and rejoin her calf.

The male manatee has no role in rearing or protecting the calf, and tends to join other manatees primarily to mate. A female in estrus becomes the focal point of a "mating herd," a group of male manatees and the female, which sometimes remains together for up to a month. The estrous female often twists and turns violently, apparently to escape her suitors. The bulls do not appear to compete for the cow in the sense that they establish defended territories around her. Rather, each bull simply attempts to remain adjacent to the female, presumably to be the first animal to mate with her. Not surprisingly, bulls sometimes collide with one another during their efforts.

Female manatees being pursued by bulls frequently swim into shoals or shallow water, possibly to prevent the males from reaching their undersides to mate. Occasionally, the cows raise their tails out of the water, slapping approaching males on the downstroke. In Florida, mating groups have often been reported as manatees in "distress" by the uninitiated observer. After a consort period, during which the bulls remain with the female, the herd breaks up. The males and pregnant females go their separate ways.

Another aspect of herd behavior involves social facilitation, a behavior pattern that is increased in pace or frequency by the behavior of other animals. This pattern is seen in many manatee activities, including feeding, resting, nuzzling, body surfing and follow-the-leader.

Manatee body surfing involves groups of manatees riding the powerful currents generated below flood dams when the gates are partly open. Sessions of body surfing can last more than an hour, with manatees repeatedly riding the currents in parallel formation. The manatees display a variety of surfing positions. The animals may simply drift downstream or may ride the currents parallel to each other, but broadside to the current; they also cut diagonally back and forth across the currents. Throughout the ride, the parallel formation is not broken, and the animals perform in a coordinated fashion. Body-surfing manatees frequently nuzzle one another and vocalize between rides.

Follow-the-leader is another form of coordinated behavior in which two or more manatees move together in single file, synchronizing all their activities, such as breathing, diving and changing direction. There does not seem to be, however, a dominant herd leader, as many individuals will take turns leading the herd. Many researchers have suggested that these forms of behavior may be considered "play," although there has not been enough information about manatee behavior to definitively support this. Whatever the classification of this activity, communication is important in synchronizing the behavior of individuals in the group. How manatees communicate is still unclear, but most researchers believe that acoustics are very important.

The daily behavior of a manatee centers around just a few activities. Six to eight hours may be spent feeding. Several more hours are occupied by resting, either alone or with other manatees. The remainder of the day is spent in any of a number of activities, including traveling; curiously investigating objects; and socializing by mouthing, rubbing against or playing with other manatees. Manatees seem to perform the same activities during the night and day, intermittently feeding and resting. Seasonally, the animals migrate in response to changing weather conditions. It seems to be an idyllic life, and it is spoiled only by the intrusion of humans with their noises, chemicals, watercraft and flood control structures.

CONSERVATION

The official minimum population size of the Florida manatee was in 1990 about 1,200 animals, with approximately half inhabiting the Atlantic coast and half the Gulf of Mexico coast of Florida and adjacent states. Given the difficulties encountered in trying to count manatees in turbid waters and areas of extensive overhanging vegetation, scientists do not know how close the minimum count is to the real population size, although a statewide manatee survey conducted on February 17–18, 1991, produced a count of nearly, 1465 animals.

Scientists from the U.S. Fish and Wildlife Service, Florida Department of Natural Resources, University of Miami and other agencies and organizations have tried to assess the number of manatees that die each year and the cause of death. Annual mortality rates have exceeded 10% of the minimum population for the past several years and are increasing each year. In 1989, a record number (174) of manatee carcasses was recovered in the southeastern United States; by September 1990, that unenviable record had already been broken and the final tally for 1990 was 216. In fact, total manatee mortality has risen an average of 5.3% each year since 1976. The two categories of mortality that have shown the most dramatic increase between 1976 and

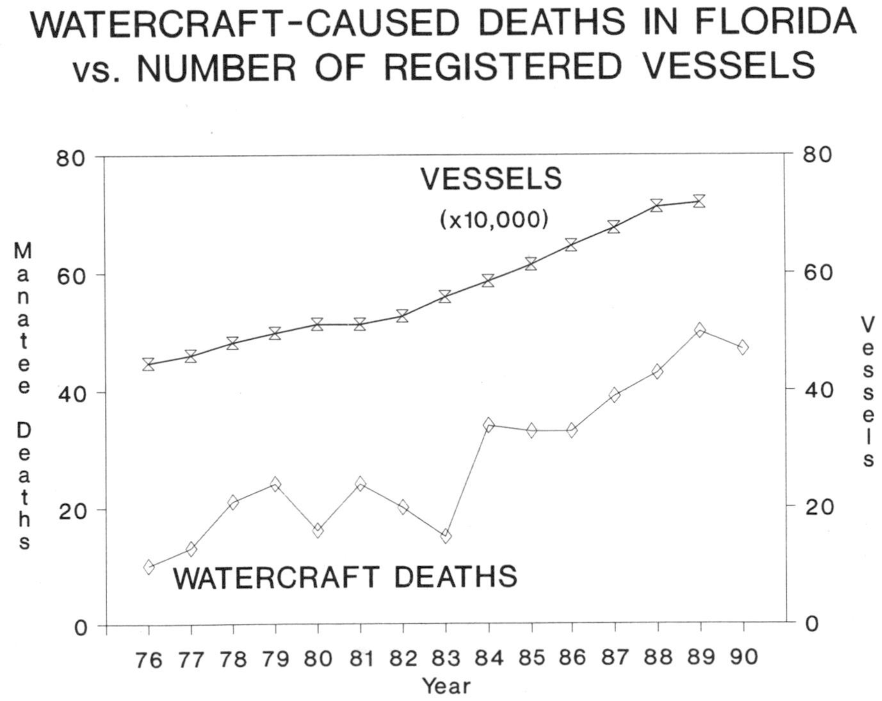
WATERCRAFT-CAUSED DEATHS IN FLORIDA
vs. NUMBER OF REGISTERED VESSELS
VESSELS
(x10,000)
WATERCRAFT DEATHS
Manatee Deaths
Vessels
0
20
40
60
80
76 77 78 79 80 81 82 83 84 85 86 87 88 89 90
Year

The rise in watercraft-related manatee deaths roughly parallels the rise in the number of registered boats in Florida. Between 1976 and mid-1990 watercraft-related mortality rose an average of 10.7% each year. Data and figure provided by Bruce B. Ackerman of the Florida Department of Natural Resources, Marine Mammals Section

mid-1990 have been watercraft-related deaths (up an average of 10.7% annually) and dependent-calf mortality (up over 11%, on average, each year).

Natural causes of mortality include disease and parasitism. Severe health problems arise after manatees are exposed to cold weather. There are no documented accounts of predation on manatees by sharks, alligators or crocodiles, but it is possible that such predation does occur infrequently. Human-related mortality occurs for a number of reasons, including collisions with watercraft (the primary human-related cause of death); crushing in flood control structures and navigation locks; shooting manatees for food or simply as vandalism; illegally tying ropes around manatee flippers to ride the animals and leaving the ropes in place, causing septicemia (a systemic infection; blood poisoning); entanglement in fishing gear; ingestion of fish hooks or trash; and possibly pollution, since manatees have been found with extremely high levels of copper (which has been used in herbicides) in their tissues.

High and increasing mortality would not be so bad if natality were sufficient to offset the number of dead animals. Sadly, recent calf counts around certain power plants (such as the Florida Power & Light Company plant mentioned earlier) have suggested that the annual birth rate for at least some groups of manatees in Florida may be declining and is already less than the mortality rate. To accurately assess what is happening to the Florida manatee

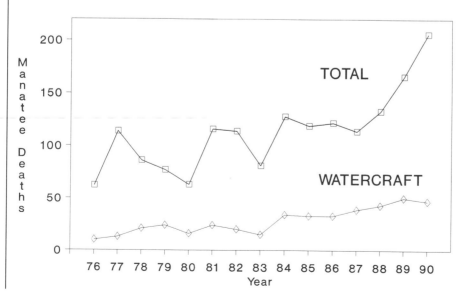

MANATEE DEATHS IN FLORIDA
1976-1990

Although there have been certain years when manatee mortality decreased relative to the previous year, the overall rate of increase in manatee mortality averages 5.3% annually. Between 1976 and mid-1990, watercraft-related mortality rose steadily at an average rate of 10.7% a year, roughly parallel to the rise in number of registered boats in Florida. Data and figure provided by Bruce B. Ackerman of the Florida Department of Natural Resources, Marine Mammals Section

population, better data are needed regarding such factors as age-specific reproductive potential and age-specific mortality. Lacking such data, it makes sense to view the situation for the Florida manatee as no less than critical and requiring immediate action to reduce human-caused manatee mortality.

Some of the efforts to protect the manatee and its habitat are described later in the chapter on conservation.

THE
ANTILLEAN
MANATEE

Until 1986, the Antillean manatee (*Trichechus manatus manatus*) and the Florida manatee (*Trichechus manatus latirostris*) were considered by most biologists to be a single species (*T. manatus*, the Caribbean or West Indian manatee). In 1934, Robert T. Hatt of the American Museum of Natural History named the two subspecies of the West Indian manatee, but it was not until the 1980s that sufficient skeletal materials (especially skulls) were available to permit Daryl Domning and Lee-Ann Hayek to distinguish the subspecies. The Florida manatee is found in the continental United States, and the Antillean manatee is found throughout the greater Caribbean area (including Mexico and southern Texas) and northeastern South America.

*The Antillean manatee (*Trichechus manatus manatus*), resembles its Florida relative. Features of the skull and current distribution differentiate the two subspecies.* Drawing by Leslie Ward

UNITED STATES

MEXICO

CUBA

HAITI DOM REP

BELIZE

GUATEMALA HONDURAS

EL SALVADOR NICARAGUA

COSTA RICA PANAMA

PUERTO RICO

ATLANTIC   OCEAN

VENEZUELA

GUYANA

COLOMBIA

SURINAME FR GUI

EQUATOR

ECUADOR

EQUATOR

SOUTH AMERICA

BRAZIL

PERU

BOLIVIA

CHILE

PARAGUAY

Range of the Antillean manatee.
Drawing by Leslie Ward

The Antillean manatee's size and shape are nearly the same as the Florida manatee's. Maximum lengths and weights for the Antillean subspecies have not been documented, but it is likely that they may reach a body length in excess of 3.5 meters (11.5 feet) and weight of 1,000 kilograms (2,200 pounds). Average adult body length is probably on the order of 3 meters (about 10 feet) and a weight of 500 kilograms (1,200 pounds). Typical of all manatees, the body shape is cylindrical, tapered at both ends. The Antillean manatee has fingernails and many other characteristics similar to those of the Florida manatee, described in the previous chapter. Externally, the subspecies are not distinguishable. The distinction is based on an extensive quantitative analysis of cranial characteristics.

The distribution and abundance of the Antillean subspecies have only been spottily documented in recent years, and much of the existing information may be out of date. Lynn Lefebvre of the U.S. Fish and Wildlife Service and her colleagues detailed in a 1989 publication the biogeography of the West Indian manatee, and much of the following material is based on their extremely comprehensive overview. From the available information one can conclude that the manatee is not evenly distributed in its greater Caribbean range. Similarly, population density is not uniform. By all accounts, the present range is smaller than the historic range, and the population is lower. Unfortunately, the historic data are not good enough to tell us how much lower the number is today, even if we had complete survey data. The population has been subjected to intensive hunting and, even though the Antillean manatee is protected in all countries in which it is found, the laws are often difficult to enforce for a variety of reasons, including lack of enforcement personnel.

The existing data clearly relate the unevenness of manatee distribution to the patchiness of suitable habitat. Manatees require both vegetation (sea grasses, freshwater plants) for food and a source of fresh water. Highest population densities are found where these essential resources exist. Seasonal shifts in local abundance seem, at least in some areas, to correlate with the rainy season. Manatees go up river (as long as the current is not too strong) when water levels are high and move downstream when water levels drop in the dry season. Unfortunately, environmental conditions that result in higher population densities make the manatees easier prey for hunters.

Antillean manatees live in a number of countries. Since the status of the subspecies varies with location, each country is considered separately in this chapter. Some of the research to date has involved local scientists working closely with members of the U.S. Fish and Wildlife Service's Sirenia Project.

Brazil

Historic and recent manatee distribution in Brazil is patchy and related to food availability and, at the southern end of the range, environmental temperature. A survey of the Brazilian coast for manatees was conducted in 1980. Historically, the Antillean manatee occurred as far south as Espiritu Santo (20° S latitude), approximately the location of the 24° C mean annual isotherm (areas having the same mean temperatures). Manatees are sensitive to cold weather, and seasonal movements are clearly related to ambient air and water temperatures. The primary areas of manatee distribution in Brazil are (from the north): Amapá state from the Ro Oiapoque on the border of French Guiana south to Cabo Norte; Maranhão state, including the Ro Mearim; Ro Grande do Norte; Paraiba, Pernambuco, Alagoas, Sergipe and Bahia states, as far south as Baía de Todos os Santos (but not in the Baía itself). Cabo Norte is on the north side of the broad mouth of the Amazon River, where the Amazonian manatee (*T. inunguis*) also occurs, and Daryl Domning has pointed out that the Cabo Norte region may be the only place in the world where two species of manatees coexist. Manatees here feed on a variety of vegetation, including seagrasses and floating, emergent and bank vegetation.

Hunting of the Antillean manatees may still occur infrequently in parts of Brazil (Paraiba, for example). Both the Antillean and the Amazonian manatees have been protected there since 1967.

French Guiana

Circumstantial evidence indicates that manatees occur in some coastal rivers, but surveys have not been conducted in this country. Coastal habitat is apparently unsuitable for manatees.

Surinam

Manatees are found in most of the coastal rivers and adjacent mangrove and freshwater swamps and may occur up to 60 kilometers (37 miles) inland from the ocean. There have been no recent, nationwide surveys for manatees. Some speculate that increasing power boat traffic in some rivers may become a threat to the manatee, as it is in Florida. Additionally, manatees in Surinam may be taken accidentally in fishing nets.

Guyana

Manatees are found in most, if not all, of the coastal rivers, including the Canje, Abary, Courantyne, Berbice, Demerara, Essequibo, Pomeroon and Arapiako. The animals feed on a variety of marine and freshwater vegetation, and manatees in Guyana have been used as agents for removal of aquatic plants from waterways for decades. Systematic surveys of manatee abundance have not been conducted, but they seem to be less abundant than in the past. Protected since 1956, manatees in Guyana still die in fishing nets, and they may be struck by motorboats.

Trinidad

Manatees are found in Nariva Swamp and perhaps in the North Oropuche River of this island nation, but the manatee population size is unknown. The swamp itself may be subjected to development that could disrupt the habitat that supports manatees. The animals apparently move toward the coast during the dry season, following a pattern seen in other parts of the range of the Antillean manatee. Intentional manatee hunting probably does not occur, but an occasional animal may become entangled, and drown, in fishing nets in the North Oropuche River.

Venezuela

Thomas J. O'Shea of the U.S. Fish and Wildlife Service and his colleagues conducted aerial and interview surveys to assess manatee distribution in Venezuela in 1986. They found that, apparently due to lack of suitable habitat, manatees were not found along the extensive Caribbean coastline of this country. Some manatees are found in Lago de Maracaibo in the west, but most manatees in Venezuela are found to the east along Golfo de Paria and in the extensive Orinoco River system, where a substantial manatee population may exist. As in other countries, the manatee has been heavily hunted and there are no good estimates of historic or recent population levels. Even though the population size is unknown, and has undoubtedly been reduced, manatee status in Venezuela may not be as grave as in other populations of Antillean manatees, because hunting pressure seems to have decreased in response to law enforcement, education programs and the lack of a market for manatee meat.

Colombia

Although a systematic survey for manatees is lacking, small numbers are found primarily in the Río Magdalena and the Río Atrato. Even though they are protected by national regulation, manatees continue to be hunted because their meat brings a high price on the black market. The number of manatees taken for food is unknown.

Panama

Recent (1987) aerial surveys by Thomas J. O'Shea and others assessed the distribution and status of manatees in Panama, particularly in the Río San San. Interviews with fishermen and others supplemented the aerial survey data. In Bocas del Toro (historically an area of high manatee abundance) manatees were found in a number of rivers in small groups (up to six animals), with over 15% of the animals being calves. Outside Bocas del Toro, manatee sightings were relatively rare. Some other areas inhabited by manatees were Gatun Lake and areas in Veranguas and Colón. Generally, manatees were found in riverine and estuarine waters, perhaps as a means of avoiding marine predators, such as sharks. The maximum number of manatees sighted during a single aerial survey was 13. The scientists estimated that between 42 and 72 manatees exist today in Panama.

The few remaining Panamanian manatees are hunted illegally by poachers using rifles or harpoons. Coastal development and habitat destruction further threaten the manatees. Efforts to manage fisheries have prohibited use of gill nets in rivers, which, if used, would probably accidentally kill some animals as they do elsewhere in their range. The scientists concluded that "the best hope for maintaining manatee populations as part of the Panamanian fauna lies in locally directed conservation efforts."

In 1984, Gene Montgomery, working for the Smithsonian Tropical Research Institute, reported that a manatee had been spotted repeatedly below the last lock (Miraflores Locks) of the Panama Canal. Thus, it appears that at least one manatee has entered the Pacific through the Panama Canal. However, Luis Mou Sue and coworkers found no manatees along the Pacific coast in their 1987 surveys.

A lithograph from about 1800 shows a manatee (bottom) with several pinnipeds (the group that contains seals, sea lions and walruses). Zoologists at that time considered the manatee to be an unusual, subtropical form of walrus. Photograph by David Williams

Vauthier del. Couché fils dir. Mougeot sc.

1. Le grand Lamantin du Kamtschatka — 2. Le Lamantin.

A lithograph from about 1800 shows three Sirenians. The top figure is a Steller's sea cow, the middle one is simply called a sea cow and the bottom figure is of an American manatee (species unknown). The anatomy is extremely inaccurate, with no split tail fluke for Steller's sea cow and a hog-nosed manatee. Photograph by David Williams

Skulls of the various species of Sirenia showing the difference in the degree of rostral deflection, or downward slope, of the front of the skull. The Amazonian manatee (top right) shows little deflection because it feeds at the surface. The dugong skull (bottom left) has a markedly deflected rostrum, appropriate for a bottom feeder.

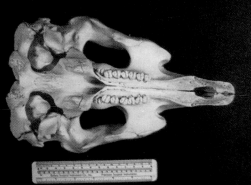

Clockwise from top left: The tooth rows in the jaw of a Florida manatee. New teeth are formed throughout the manatee's life and move from back to front as the older teeth are worn down by the gritty vegetation the manatees eat. Photograph by Daniel K. Odell

The skull of an Amazonian manatee. Photograph by Daryl P. Domning

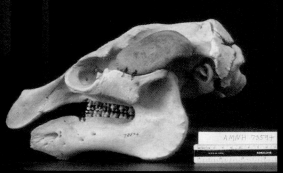

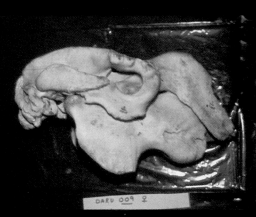

The skull of a dugong. Small protruding tusks have growth layers, permitting scientists to tell the age of individual dugongs. Photograph by Daryl P. Domning

Daryl Domning holds a dugong skull. Resting on the table is the skull of a Steller's sea cow. The size and degree of rostral deflection of the skulls is very different. The Steller's sea cow also lacked teeth. Photograph by Chip Clark.

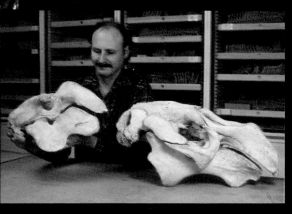

Florida manatees swim near hydrilla, an exotic aquatic plant, at Crystal River.
Photograph by William A. Szelistowski

A group of Florida manatees (top) and a resting manatee (below). Photographs by Patrick M. Rose

Swimming Florida manatees. Photograph by Patrick M. Rose

Florida manatee in clear water. Note the transmitter belt around the animal's tail stock. Photograph by Patrick M. Rose

Manatee surfacing for air. Photograph by Patrick M. Rose

Resting manatee. Photograph by Patrick M. Rose

Pregnant female manatee. Calves may weigh up to about 27 kilograms (60 pounds) at birth. Photograph by Patrick M. Rose

A female manatee and her calf swim together. The female has several deep cuts in her back as a result of a collision with a motorboat propeller. Photograph by Patrick M. Rose

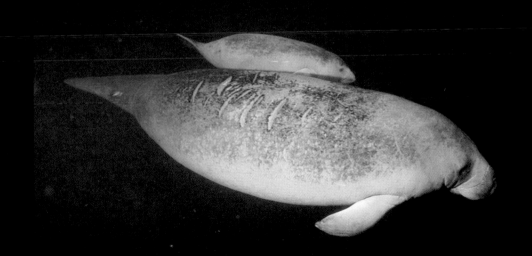

Mother and calf swim together. There are pro-peller-inflicted cuts on the mother's back.
Photograph by John E. Reynolds III

A Florida manatee and her calf. Photograph by Patrick M. Rose

Surfacing manatee. Photograph by Patrick M. Rose

Manatees that aggregate at Crystal River in Florida in winter enjoy two benefits: warm water and abundant food. These animals feed primarily on hydrilla. Photographs courtesy of U.S. Fish and Wildlife Service, Sirenia Project

Resting manatees. A researcher can be seen in the photograph at top. Photographs by Patrick M. Rose

Costa Rica

Manatees are apparently rare in Costa Rica as a result of historic hunting pressure. No recent surveys have been conducted. Favorable habitat for manatees exists along the northeastern and southeastern coasts, and Tortuguero National Park is an important protected area for the few remaining manatees. According to Lefebvre and her colleagues, "Enforcement of recent protective legislation . . ., establishment of reserves, and a dying interest in hunting linked to manatee scarcity . . . provide the best prospects for the species' recovery in Costa Rica."

Nicaragua

Nicaragua has extensive coastal seagrass beds and coastal lagoons that would seem ideal manatee habitat. However, there are virtually no data on manatee distribution or abundance in this country. Although hunting of manatees for food occurred in the past, levels of take have been low in recent years.

Honduras

Aerial surveys and interview data indicate that manatees are found in Honduras where the habitat is suitable (eastern and western regions of the country), but additional surveys are needed. Three primary areas are occupied by manatees: rivers and lagoons found to the west of La Ceiba, around La Mosquitia (eastern Honduras), and rivers east of Trujillo. Apparently hunting (by harpoons) and intentional and accidental gill netting of manatees are widespread, and adequate law enforcement is necessary to protect the species. Hunting pressure may have led the manatees in Honduras to become nocturnal. Recent information suggests that manatee numbers may be rising as hunting pressure has diminished.

Guatemala

Manatees are found in rivers and coastal areas, but their numbers are apparently quite low. Hunting still occurs, and manatee meat may be sold in some markets. Interestingly, Guatemala apparently has the first designated manatee reserve in Central or South America, the Biotopo Para La Conservación del Manati Chocon-Machacas at El Golfete.

Belize

In contrast to the situation in most of the countries in Central and South America bordering the Caribbean, surveys for manatees in Belize are both relatively extensive and recent. Although Belize is only a small country, its coast provides excellent manatee habitat, and the animals have been seen along the entire coast, especially at river mouths. Five areas are frequented by manatees:

Four Mile Lagoon and the lower New River; the lower Belize River; cays off Belize City; Southern Lagoon; and Placentia Lagoon. Thomas O'Shea and Lex Salisbury did the most recent surveys (in 1989), and found, among other things, 55 manatees during one survey of Southern Lagoon. These animals may have been attracted to an upwelling freshwater spring. The counts in Southern Lagoon are the highest known for manatees in a specific location in the Caribbean; this fact, combined with relatively abundant calves (10.6% of the total animals sighted) and other factors, led O'Shea and Salisbury to conclude that "Belize remains one of the last strongholds for this species in this part of the world."

A combination of factors, including presence of suitable habitat, low human population, lack of traditional manatee hunting, small gillnet fisheries and development of conservation and education programs conducted by the Belize Zoo are probably responsible for the healthy status of the manatee population. Given this excellent status, the effort to protect manatees in Belize must not be lessened. Education and law enforcement are now more important than ever.

Mexico

Some literature has stated that the northern limit of the continental distribution of the Antillean manatee is on the Gulf coast of Mexico at Nautla, Veracruz. Historically, manatees have been reported north of Veracruz and occasionally were seen along the west Texas coast. In fact, a 1989 report indicated that manatees still do occur north of Veracruz, specifically in the Palmas and Soto la Marina Rivers. A few manatees have been spotted there in small groups during the rainy, summer months. Environmental conditions (primarily temperature) have presumably limited the northern movement of manatees, and Mexican scientists feel that over-exploitation has been responsible for virtually eliminating manatees that seasonally venture north of Veracruz.

Much of the recent work on manatees in Mexico has been done by Luz del Carmen Colmenero-R. Along the Gulf coast of Mexico, manatees are relatively abundant near Alvarado in southern Veracruz and in Tabasco and Chiapas states. On the Caribbean coast, manatees are abundant in Quintana Roo, near the border with Belize in Chetumal Bay and Río Hondo. Manatees move up some rivers during the rainy season and feed on freshwater vegetation. Calving season may be synchronized with the rainy season so that calves are born when there is abundant vegetation for their mothers to eat. Manatee hunting has declined in recent decades as other fisheries (for finfish and crustaceans) have developed. Some manatee hunting and incidental take in nets still occurs, and expanded conservation and law enforcement efforts are necessary, including establishment of reserves or sanctuaries.

Cuba

In 1494, Columbus reported that freshwater springs in the Bahía de Cochinos attracted "swarms" of manatees. Manatees still exist there today. In fact, manatees occur on both coasts of Cuba in coastal habitats where they feed on sea grasses. Three areas where manatees seem to be most abundant are Golfo de Guanahacabibes, the area between Cortes and La Coloma, and at Ensenada de la Broa/Río Hatiguanico. Historically, manatees were apparently most common in rivers, but they may have changed their distribution to more marine areas, possibly due to habitat changes resulting from human activities. There are no quantitative estimates of manatee abundance in Cuba, but aerial surveys by Carlos Wotzkow (of the Museo Nacional de Historia Natural) produced a number of manatee sightings, including groups of up to 14 animals, the most sighted on a single survey.

An interesting behavior described by fishermen and others was that female manatees left their nursing calves in safe, quiet areas while they ventured out to feed. A large group of "calves" was observed in a river, supporting this claim.

In a series of interviews, researchers in Cuba found that 58% of the respondents thought that manatees had become more abundant there in recent years. Manatees (which are protected in Cuba) and sharks (which potentially could prey on manatees) have been reduced in numbers by fishing activities. Primary threats to the population include accidental entanglement in fishing nets, poaching and habitat destruction.

Haiti

The manatee population is extremely small, and its status is considered tenuous at best. Only eight manatees were counted in an aerial survey of the entire coastline conducted in 1982. Areas used by manatees are also important fishing areas, and manatees are sometimes accidentally caught in beach seines. The future of manatees in Haiti is extremely uncertain.

Dominican Republic

David and Cheryl Belitsky conducted six aerial surveys of the entire coast in 1977. The existing manatee population seemed to be concentrated on part of the north coast and on the southwest coast of the country, with the greatest manatee concentrations occurring in Bahía de Neiba and near Las Terrenas. The habitat is generally coastal marine, but there is some indication that manatees frequent river mouths and springs (probably for freshwater sources). The Belitskys saw from 2 to 30 manatees on the north coast and 1 to 11 manatees on the southwest coast. The range and abundance of manatees in the Dominican Republic have been reduced by hunting and habitat degradation. Manatees are still poached and caught accidentally in fishing nets.

Jamaica

In 1981 and 1982, P.W. Fairbairn and A. W. Haynes conducted 13 aerial surveys of the entire coast of Jamaica. Between 1 and 13 manatees were seen on each flight, primarily along the south coast, west of Kingston. They are found in both marine and freshwater habitats and presumably feed on vegetation in both habitats. Manatees are illegally taken in Jamaica and the meat sold, and some are accidentally killed in fishing nets. James Powell documented manatees stripping the flesh from fish that had been caught in gill nets, one of the few documented occurrences of manatee carnivory in the wild. It would appear that the manatee population is quite small and in need of complete protection if the species is to survive in Jamaica.

Puerto Rico

Work on manatees in Puerto Rico has been much more extensive than in most countries where the Antillean manatee is found, because they come under the jurisdiction of the U.S. Endangered Species Act of 1973. James Powell and his colleagues conducted 10 aerial surveys in 1978-79 and Galen Rathbun and his colleagues conducted 12 surveys in 1985-86. Most of the manatees were seen on the eastern and south-central coasts, and none on the northwest coast. Powell saw from 11 to 51 manatees per survey and Rathbun saw 20 to 62 manatees per survey. Manatees tend to congregate in the vicinity of the Roosevelt Roads Naval Station on the eastern end of the island. Here manatees have been observed apparently drinking freshwater from the base sewage discharge. As in other areas around the Caribbean, manatee distribution is not uniform and is most likely related to the distribution of freshwater sources and seagrass beds.

Several manatee carcasses have been examined by the carcass salvage program operated by the U.S. Fish and Wildlife Service. At least three manatees were killed in nets, and one was killed by a boat.

Virgin Islands

The only reports of manatees in the Virgin Islands are recent (1988). In mid-November of that year, a single adult manatee was seen at least twice in the harbor of Charlotte Amalie, St. Thomas. Later that month a dead manatee, apparently killed as a result of a watercraft collision, was found there. This animal may have reached the Virgin Islands by crossing deep water between there and Puerto Rico.

Bahamas

Sightings of manatees in the Bahamas are rare at best, and the country has not been thoroughly surveyed. A manatee was recorded at the Bimini Islands in 1904, and one was seen alive at West End, Grand Bahama in 1975. A dead manatee was found near Freeport, Grand Bahama later in 1975. Daryl Domning subsequently examined the skull and determined that it was from a Florida manatee and not an Antillean manatee, suggesting that the animal may have crossed the Gulf Stream from the Florida coast. Manatees might also enter the Bahamas from the south. Although the Bahamas have extensive seagrass beds, lack of ample freshwater sources may limit the manatees' presence. However, thorough aerial surveys should be conducted to determine just how common, or uncommon, manatees are in the Bahamas.

The Antillean manatee is unevenly distributed throughout the Caribbean basin with the exception of the Lesser Antilles, where it existed historically but has not been seen in recent times. The patchiness of the distribution is related to suitable habitat (seagrasses and/or freshwater vegetation, freshwater and sheltered areas). Habitat destruction or alteration and continued take either through poaching or accidental killing in nets place a heavy burden on the Antillean manatee. It is clear that extensive protection and enforcement of existing laws are necessary. There are several places (Mexico, Belize, Venezuela) where the Antillean manatee is relatively abundant or where large amounts of suitable habitat still exist. These areas should receive ample protection to ensure that the subspecies can continue to exist.

THE
WEST AFRICAN
MANATEE

It has been said that, if a West Indian manatee and a West African manatee lay side-by-side, even an expert would be hard pressed to distinguish between the two animals. They are about the same size and shape, and possess the same wrinkled skin and sparse white hair. Actually, biologists familiar with the appearance of both species (either directly or from photographs) have noted that the West African manatee can be distinguished fairly easily because the eyes tend to protrude somewhat, the snout is blunter (almost pug-nosed), and the body is less robust. Also, the skull bones of the two species differ; for example, the rostrum of the West African species is deflected downward less than that of the West Indian species. The degree of deflection relates to food habits, and the relative lack of bottom vegetation available to *T. senegalensis* makes a downward-deflected rostrum less valuable. The general morphological similarity is not surprising, considering that some paleontologists feel the West African species arose when wandering West Indian manatees crossed the Atlantic less than 5 million years ago. Similar environmental conditions on both sides of the Atlantic did not provide evolutionary pressure for either of the two groups to adapt and change significantly, relative to one another.

Because their habitats are generally similar, the West Indian and West African manatees might be expected to have similar habitat requirements, physiological tolerances and behavior. The available data suggest that this expectation is correct. James Powell, for example, reported in 1985 that

Skull of the West African manatee, Trichechus senegalensis. *There is less downward deflection of the rostrum than in the West Indian species, reflecting a lack of bottom vegetation in the environment.* Drawing by Leslie Ward

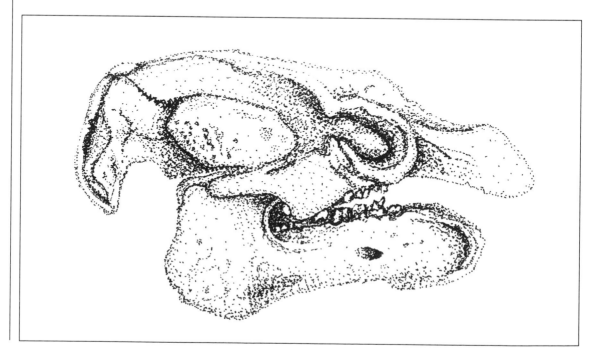

A West African manatee. This species resembles the West Indian manatee but is less robust and has a blunter snout and more protuberant eyes. Drawing by Leslie Ward

manatees in Gambia, like West Indian manatees, are found along the coast, in estuaries and far up rivers. They require calm waters, access to freshwater and adequate food. In estuaries, they frequent sources of freshwater. In general, West African manatees appear to prefer quiet coastal areas, large rivers, lagoons and connected lakes. As with other living sirenians, water temperature is an important determinant of acceptable habitat, as the West African manatee's distribution seems to be limited to waters warmer than 18° C (about 64° F). Breeding appears to occur year-round, although James Powell has suggested that changes in food availability during the rainy season may lead to some seasonality in breeding.

In the warm coastal and riverine waters of West Africa, aquatic vascular plants support herbivores such as the manatee. Where submerged or floating aquatic plants are sparse or absent, manatees may forage on plants growing on the bank or even on mangrove leaves. In a couple of instances, West African manatees have been reported (based on stomach contents of butchered animals) to feed on clams, something that West Indian manatees also have been reported to do in Puerto Rico.

Like the West Indian manatees, West African manatees have few predators. Although crocodiles and sharks kill some manatees in Africa, the only significant predator is man.

Although there are substantial similarities between the West Indian and West African manatees, the two species differ in at least two important ways: in the amount of available data and the impact that humans have had on each species. In fact, the species of sirenian about which the least information is known is the West African manatee. For each of the other living sirenians, a center where teams of scientists has addressed the anatomy, behavior and ecology of the species has been established. For example, the primary center of dugong research is based at Townsville, Australia, where George Heinsohn, Helene Marsh, and others have worked; for Amazonian manatees the Projeto

Peixe-Boi in Manaus, Brazil has benefitted from the efforts of Daryl Domning, Robin Best and many other scientists; in the United States, the Federal government's center for research on Florida manatees in Gainesville, Florida has been led most recently by Galen Rathbun and Thomas O'Shea. For the West African manatee, no such center has existed, and since 1975, only a handful of individual scientists has examined the distribution, ecology or behavior of the species. Three efforts are especially noteworthy: The eminent, late Japanese marine mammalogist Masaharu Nishiwaki and his colleagues studied the species' distribution in a few countries in 1980 and 1981; James A. Powell, Jr. who studied *Trichechus manatus* for nearly two decades (mid-1960s to mid-1980s) in Florida and parts of the Caribbean, has investigated manatee biology and management in Gambia, Ivory Coast, Nigeria, Mali, Senegal, Guinea Bissau and Cameroon since the mid-1980s; and marine mammalogist Randall R. Reeves studied manatees in Sierra Leone and Nigeria in 1986 and 1987.

There have been some anatomical studies of West African manatees and some brief accounts of manatee distribution and behavior. However, the relative lack of research using either wild or captive specimens means that there are glaring deficiencies in the data base for West African manatees. Scientists lack adequate knowledge, for example, regarding the size of the manatee population, precisely where they are located, age-specific reproduction and mortality, what the levels and causes of mortality are and the social behavior of the manatees. Imagine trying to conserve and manage a species that occupies a number of separate countries and for which so little information exists.

The West African manatee's wide distribution covers freshwater to coastal marine waters from Senegal to Angola, meaning that the species can be found in over a dozen countries. Interestingly enough, the current overall range of the species seems to differ little from the historical range, even though scientists estimate that the total number of manatees in Africa has decreased in the past and continues to decrease today, and that certain localized groups of manatees have been exterminated. Because the status of both manatees and knowledge about them varies from country to country, we consider them by location.

Senegal

Masaharu Nishiwaki and his colleagues considered manatee distribution and abundance in Senegal. These scientists had thought that conditions (such as lack of forage, extremely hot summer weather or high levels of industrial activity) through much of the country were not conducive to manatee survival, and interviews with local residents supported this assumption, though in one area, Lac de Cuiers, "a considerable number of animals" have been reported to exist.

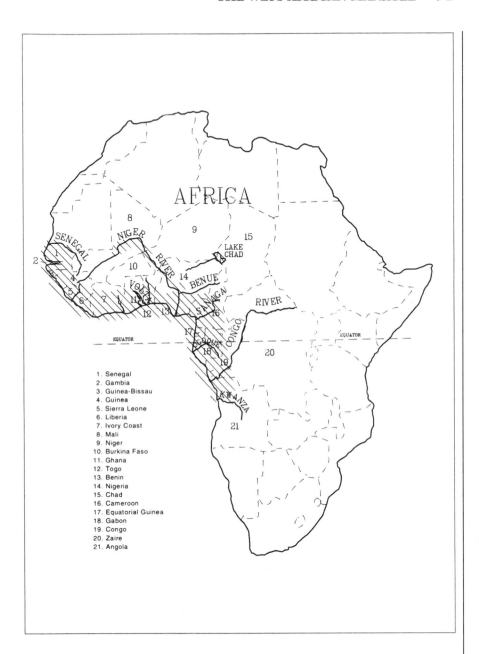

Range of the West African manatee. Drawn by Leslie Ward

1. Senegal
2. Gambia
3. Guinea-Bissau
4. Guinea
5. Sierra Leone
6. Liberia
7. Ivory Coast
8. Mali
9. Niger
10. Burkina Faso
11. Ghana
12. Togo
13. Benin
14. Nigeria
15. Chad
16. Cameroon
17. Equatorial Guinea
18. Gabon
19. Congo
20. Zaire
21. Angola

More recently, James Powell has studied manatees in Senegal. He reports that manatees are found all along the coast and that they are not uncommon in the Senegal River. They are actually found far upstream (how far is uncertain). During the annual dry season, the river falls, so manatees move downstream. Sometimes the animals get trapped by falling water levels in tributaries or lakes that connect to the Senegal River in the rainy season. The

Ministry of Water and Forests sends staff out to "bring" the isolated individual manatees back to the river. Powell reports that manatees are a top priority for protection in Senegal.

Gambia

James Powell found that manatees are widely distributed in the Gambia River basin. They occupy a variety of habitat types. In the coastal region, manatees were common in the Allahein River prior to 1974, but the population there has declined drastically due to drought and subsequent die-off of mangroves, the leaves of which form the bulk of the diet of manatees there. Along much of the coast, manatees are not common, but around Barra, they are sighted regularly, especially in the wet season.

In the lower Gambia River (Banjul to Kau-ur) manatees are observed regularly, particularly in the area between Biara Point and Bintang Bolon. In certain parts of the lower river, salinity increases have destroyed mangroves, resulting in movements of manatees to other spots where food is more abundant. Manatees are occasionally observed in the middle Gambia River region (Kau-ur to Basse Santa Su). Near Baboon Island, for example, a national park caretaker sometimes sees animals weekly during the dry season when the animals are concentrated there (December to May). Otherwise, manatees are less common in the middle river region than in the lower river. Drought has lowered water levels to the point where manatees cannot enter certain creeks or bolons (small rivers). In the upper Gambia River area (Basse Santa Su to Simenti, Senegal), shallow water and sparse shoreline vegetation apparently discourage manatee occupation. Only in the wet season can an occasional manatee be seen.

Powell concluded that manatees are not common in Gambia, but did not estimate the size of the Gambia manatee population. He found that manatees there may show daily and seasonal activity patterns; daily movements may occur in response to tides and seasonal ones in response to salinity and depth changes during the wet and dry seasons.

The government of Gambia has proposed a series of dams along the Gambia River. Such dams could cause considerable damage to manatees either directly (by crushing them in gates or locks) or indirectly (by extensively altering such features of the habitat as amount of freshwater or vegetation available). Any additional source of human-induced harm, on top of existing harvest by hunters (about two animals per year), and reduced forage due to drought, could significantly affect the status of manatees in Gambia.

Liberia, Guinea-Bissau and Guinea

Christopher Columbus apparently observed manatees off the coast of Guinea, and other old records note the presence of manatees along the coast of Liberia.

More recently, Karl R. Kranz, then of the National Zoological Park in Washington, D.C., traveled to Liberia in 1983 and interviewed residents and surveyed coastal and riverine areas for manatees, which in Liberia and in some other West African countries are called "mammy-water." Interviews suggest that some manatees can still be found in Liberia, but the species is uncommon. Apparently, manatees were commonly observed in the St. Paul River outside Monrovia, Liberia, in the 1950s and 1960s. Since construction of the Mt. Coffee hydroelectric station in 1966, manatees have not been observed in the river. Although no population estimates are available for any of these three countries, Kranz felt that manatees would be eliminated in Liberian waters unless mangrove swamp habitat is protected and a ban on manatee hunting is imposed. More recently, Powell has indicated that manatees are apparently present in most major rivers in Liberia.

In Guinea-Bissau, manatees are generally rare along the coast, but seem to be fairly common around some islands in the Bijagos Archipelago, according to Powell. They are hunted only by Senegalese fishermen, who erect platforms at freshwater seeps; when manatees come to the seeps to drink, the fishermen harpoon the animals. In 1988, a fisherman in the Bijagos was found to possess the sterna of 52 manatees he had killed. Manatee meat is still sold in markets in Guinea-Bissau.

Sierra Leone

The most recent information regarding manatees in Sierra Leone comes from Randall R. Reeves, who spent time there in late 1986 and in 1987. He did not survey the entire country, but he discovered that manatee trapping occurs commonly among the Mende people of the Pujehun and Bonthe Districts, as well as among hunters elsewhere in the country. Although Reeves and his colleagues observed no manatees, interviews with manatee hunters suggested an average annual catch, by hunters located mainly in the coastal Pujehun District, to be as high as 20 animals.

The Mende who hunt manatees assert that the animals are abundant. The Mende, in fact, would like to see fewer manatees, because they view them as pests that tear gillnets, destroy fish in the nets (by sucking meat from the fish's bodies, which has also been reported for West Indian manatees in Jamaica) and plunder rice fields. This attitude toward the manatees, together with the Mende's enjoyment of manatee meat, makes manatee hunting, using traps and nets, a popular activity within this tribe.

The types of manatee catching devices used in Sierra Leone vary from one region of the country to another. Some traps are used throughout Africa, such as the baited platforms, on which a hunter waits to spear a hungry manatee. Another type is the fence trap, where a hunter drops a trap door behind a manatee that is feeding among mangroves; in such cases the manatees are killed later using an axe. Chain nets also entrap living manatees in restricted areas, to be dispatched later. An unusual type of trap used in the Pujehun and Bonthe districts is a spear trap, in which a manatee, moving through an opening between two posts, pushes against a net that crosses the opening. This causes a spear, with the force of a heavy log behind it, to be driven deep into the animal, effectively tethering it until the hunters arrive. Manatees are also caught in nets made of strong twine, both deliberately and incidentally.

Interviews of manatee hunters by Reeves and his colleagues demonstrated that catches by some individuals can be as high as 15 per year. One hunter claimed to have taken over 200 in his lifetime. However, most of the hunters are old men who claim that manatee hunting is less common today than in the past. In most cases, the hunters did not attribute this to any reduction in numbers of manatees. Despite protective legislation, manatee meat is openly consumed and even sold in markets in Sierra Leone, with an animal bringing about US $20 in the Kambia District.

Reeves and his associates estimated the distribution of manatees in Sierra Leone, based both on interviews with villagers and on presence of manatee traps and nets. Apparently manatees are captured near the mouths of both the Great Scarcies and Little Scarcies rivers, and they are present as far up the Great Scarcies as Rokupr. Hunters also trap manatees near the head of the Bunce River. Other rivers where manatees are reported to be observed or trapped in Sierra Leone include the Sherbo system and a creek near Rogberay on the north side of the Sierra Leone River. Manatees are also said to occupy Lakes Mape and Mabesi. One interesting feature of manatee distribution in Sierra Leone is that manatees move into upriver areas most abundantly in the flood season, starting in June and July. Not unexpectedly, most manatee hunting occurs in the wet season.

No estimates exist for the manatee population in Sierra Leone. Reeves and his coworkers felt that, although there is potential for overexploitation of manatees in Sierra Leone, the habitat there should be able to support the species for some time. The scientists warned, however, that incidental take in developing fisheries could be a major problem for manatees in Sierra Leone.

Ivory Coast

Nishiwaki and his colleagues reported numerous manatees occupying a variety of habitats in the Ivory Coast. Subsequently a long-term program of manatee research was initiated in 1986, supported by Wildlife Conservation International and the International Union for the Conservation of Nature and Natural Resources (now called the World Conservation Union) to promote public awareness and research. The research involves systematic surveys, radio tracking, interviews with villagers and examination of carcasses. Interestingly, manatees on which radio transmitters are placed are caught using traditional manatee traps; the scientists (led by James Powell) have found that the traps are very effective for capturing manatees unharmed—the traps caught five manatees in eight nights for the scientists. In a letter to *Sirenews*, Powell described how the trap operates:

> These traps are constructed from a number of wooden stakes stuck in the bottom and secured together with vine. The stakes are placed to form a small semi-circle (2.5 x 1 m) open at one end. A sliding door of sharpened stakes is placed on the open end. The door is held open by a system of smaller stakes which are balanced together to act as a trigger mechanism. The trap itself is usually placed in water about one meter deep. The trap is then baited nightly with fresh cassava peels thrown randomly inside the trap. When the manatee enters to eat the cassava, he accidentally pushes the trigger stick and the door falls.

Scientists have employed another traditional method used by hunters to catch the animals as well. A large meshed (about 75 centimeters or about 30 inches) net is stretched across a stream or near an area frequented by manatees. The mesh size allows only a manatee's head and flippers to pass forward; when the animal backs up or tries to free itself, it becomes more entangled.

The tagged animals are often found alone, but they seem to congregate in certain locations in groups of 25–30 during the rainy season. Powell is uncertain why these groups form. He has also found that the manatees travel extensively (30–40 kilometers, or 18–25 miles, per day) through the lagoons and rivers. In Ivory Coast waters, manatees feed on emergent vegetation and sometimes on fruit that falls from trees into the water.

Although manatees appear to be common in Ivory Coast waters, there is not a good estimate of the population size. The opinion of Nishiwaki and his associates was there may be "several thousands," but Powell feels that there are "three hundred at most." Native hunting, using the efficient traps described above, accounts for an undetermined number (maybe 20) of manatee deaths each year.

Ghana

Manatees in Ghana have been reported to inhabit the coast and parts of the Volta River system. In 1980-81, however, Nishiwaki and his coworkers acquired little information about manatee sightings or captures in Ghana. Since manatee capture is prohibited, it is likely that catches simply are not reported. Population estimates are not available, but it appears that manatees are uncommon in Ghana.

Togo and Benin

No data could be found, but Nishiwaki and his associates felt that absence of major rivers in these countries suggested that manatees would not be present. Along the northern border of Benin are the Niger and Mekrou Rivers, where manatees were once considered abundant. Uncontrolled local hunting was thought to have exterminated manatees in this area but Powell has received reports that they are still present. Along the coasts of both countries, manatees have been sighted recently.

Niger and Mali

Manatees have been observed far up the Niger River; reports exist of manatees 2,000 kilometers (about 1,240 miles) upstream, at Segou, Mali and Powell has recent reports from Malian fishermen that manatees have penetrated the Niger River as far as Guinea. Nishiwaki felt that a considerable number of manatees occupy the inland Niger Delta, and that manatees are present in the area of Niamey, Niger. On the other hand, R. Poche wrote of the manatee in the report "Niger's Threatened Park W" that "as a result of uncontrolled slaughter, it is now extinct" in that area (although Powell has a recent account to the contrary). Poche went on to describe a village chief who kept a manatee skull as a memento of former times. The number of manatees in Niger and Mali is unknown.

Chad

Scientists have debated whether manatees exist in Chad, specifically in Lake Chad. Publications in the 1970s claimed that manatees did not inhabit Lake Chad. James Powell, however, indicated in 1989 that reliable sources had informed him of the presence of manatees, at least in tributaries of the lake, and he plans to try to document their presence there.

Nigeria

Nishiwaki and his associates concluded after their 1980–81 surveys that "the most abundant distribution of manatees is in the Niger River and its tributaries and associated swamps." Dr. Sylvia Sykes, a zoologist who worked in Nigeria in the early 1970s, however, suggested that manatees were found only in "limited numbers" in the Niger, Benue and Cross rivers, and James Powell feels that Sykes' assessment is accurate today. Manatees can also be found in tributaries of those rivers.

Manatees are reported to be abundant (a few hundred individuals) in Lake Kainji, along the Niger River. In a 1987 letter to *Sirenews*, Randall Reeves noted that the dam that formed Lake Kainji has prevented manatees there from mixing with manatees downstream and that villagers use a variety of traps and other gear to harvest manatees in the lake and nearby rivers. One village on the northeast corner of the lake may take three to four manatees a year. An unusual capture method employed by hunters in the area involved a line rigged with several hundred large hooks. In the dry season, hunters anchor the line on shore, and then string it across the Niger River, with the hooks suspended just above the bottom, where they snag passing manatees. Although manatees may be present in Lake Kainji, the hydroelectric dam itself poses a threat to their existence. As many as six manatees have been killed by this structure in a single day.

No good population estimate exists for manatees in Nigeria. It is certain, however, that local tribes, including the Kabawa observed by Sykes, harvest manatees for food. It has also been alleged that Nigerian hunters may cross into neighboring Cameroon to take manatees there.

Cameroon

Although manatees have been reported to be rare in Cameroon, recent work by James Powell and Yale graduate student Melissa M. Grigione has indicated that, at least in some areas, manatees may be fairly common; for example, they thrive in estuaries and the lower reaches of rivers in southwestern Cameroon, near Korup. The animals ascend the Cross River from Nigeria to at least Mamfe in Cameroon. They are found in all major rivers along the coast including the Ndian River (Korup Region), where they are sometimes seen in small groups of about one-half dozen individuals during the rainy season, and the Ede Region contains an important manatee population. In northern Cameroon, manatees in the Benue River (a tributary of the Niger River) may enter Lake Levé in Chad in the rainy season.

According to Powell, manatees in Cameroon are hunted in some areas for ceremonial purposes, and are also harvested by transient Nigerian fishermen. Although no quantitative data on the manatee population are available, it seems that hunting pressure is decreasing. Cameroon has strict laws to prevent killing of manatees but the practice continues.

Equatorial Guinea

No data regarding manatees are available. Manatees have been sighted in coastal waters from Cameroon to the Congo, so it is likely that some animals may be found along the coast of Equatorial Guinea.

Gabon

Manatees, called *manga* in Gabon, may be common there, but population estimates based on extensive research are not available. Nishiwaki and his coworkers reported that manatees were common in the Ogoúe River, in interconnected lakes between Port-Gentil and Lambarené, and in southern coastal lagoons, including Nkomi, near Omboúe, and Ndogo, near Sette

Cama. Although hunters harvest manatees in Gabon, the country's relatively small human population and extensive rain-forest habitat could support a large number of manatees. Scientists have even ventured a guess that several thousand manatees might inhabit Gabon waters, but this figure is not supported by adequate surveys.

Congo and Zaire

No estimates of manatee abundance exist for this region. Manatees have been reported to be abundant in the lower regions of the Congo River. They have also been reported from the Uele and Mbomu Rivers. A 1942 report considered the manatee population in Zaire to be diminished. Recent reports led Powell to suggest that there may be a sizable population of manatees in Zaire, particularly in the lower reaches of the Congo and the associated seasonally flooded lakes. Manatees are also likely to be found far up the Congo and its tributaries.

Angola

The status and distribution of manatees in Angola are uncertain. The Kwanza River has been suggested, but not confirmed, as the southernmost area occupied by the West African manatee.

In 1983 and 1985, Thomas Carr visited Angola and made a number of observations regarding manatees there. He noted that manatees were reported to be "common" in the areas he visited (mainly in northern Angola around the Kwanza River), and that all local people knew what manatees were. In fact, the people had a high regard for manatee meat, which they obtained by harpooning animals that became entangled in nets at night. Crocodiles, too, were reported to eat small manatees in Angola. Interestingly, calves were reportedly seen year-round; manatees were said to exist in both salt- and freshwater locations, and manatees co-existed with hippopotami in some areas.

The preceding accounts demonstrate that in the countries comprising the West African manatee's range, there is variability in the number of animals present, the quality of the available habitat, the nature and extent of human harvest and the quality of data available. If the species is to be conserved, considerably more information is needed and international cooperation must be sought.

In some regions, conservation of West African manatees may be particularly difficult. In the northern parts of the species' range, manatee hunting may be a means of survival for people threatened by starvation as a result of the Sahelian drought, among other things. In other parts of West African, manatee hunting is a valued tradition that incidentally provides considerable amounts of delicious food. The idea of preservation of the manatees and of manatee habitat may not be priorities for people in these circumstances.

THE AMAZONIAN MANATEE

The Amazonian manatee (*Trichechus inunguis*) is the smallest of the living manatees, with the largest recorded specimen measuring only 2.8 meters (9.2 feet) in length. Maximum body weight is not known, but one large individual captured in Ecuador weighed 480 kilograms (1,056 pounds). Thus, the Amazonian manatee is both shorter and more slender than its relatives. It also typically bears distinctive white or pink patches on the belly and chest and animals older than newborns have smooth skin. Other, less obvious characteristics that distinguish the species from other manatees are lack of nails on the pectoral flippers, longer flippers, smaller teeth, and a longer, narrower rostrum (anterior part of the skull) relative to other species of manatees. At the cellular level, the Amazonian manatee is also distinctive, since it has 56 chromosomes, compared with only 48 for *Trichechus manatus*; the number of chromosomes for *Trichechus senegalensis* is not known.

The Amazonian manatee's appearance is not its only distinctive feature. The species is the only sirenian confined in its distribution to freshwater.

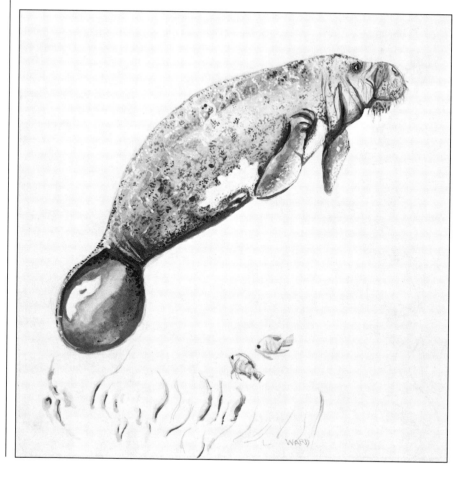

The Amazonian manatee is smaller than its relatives. Note also the lack of nails on the flippers, and light belly patches, the latter being present on most Amazonian and a few Florida manatees. Drawing by Leslie Ward

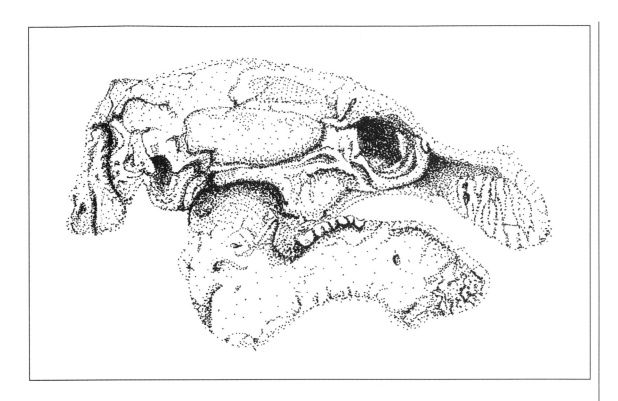

Skull of the Amazonian manatee, Trichechus inunguis. Drawing by Leslie Ward

Amazonian manatees live in the Amazon basin, occupying rivers in Brazil (the Amazon, as well as tributaries such as the Tocantins, Xingu, Tapajó, Nhamundã, Madeira, Negro and Branco), along the Brazil-Guyana border (Takatu River), in Colombia (the Amazon, Putumayo, Caqueta and lower Apaporis), in Peru (the Napo, Tigre, Marañon, Samiria, Pacaya Ucayali, and Huallago) and in Ecuador (lagoons near the Río Aguarico and the Río Cuyabeno).

The preferred habitat of the Amazonian manatee is relatively well documented. They are most abundant in floodplain lakes and channels in white-water river systems. The water in such lakes may appear dark because the silt has settled out, but it is not true "black water" (i.e., characterized by low pH). Chemically the water they favor is white water (less acidic) and high in nutrients. They prefer water temperatures probably ranging from about 25° C to 30° C (77° F–86° F) and areas with abundant vegetation.

Manatees inhabiting such areas have been reported in the past to form large herds. Today, these groups are unusual, but manatees may be seen feeding in small, loosely organized groups of four to eight individuals. In the wild, the manatees' shy behavior, their ability to remain submerged for up to 14 minutes and the dark waters they occupy have all contributed to a lack of information about the social behavior of the species. Observations of captive

Range of the Amazonian manatee. Drawn by Leslie Ward

Amazonian manatees, however, suggest that they behave in ways similar to their better-studied relative in Florida. For example, they clasp each other with their pectoral flippers and roll together in the water; they engage in sex play; they use high-pitched squeals and squeaks (6–8 kilohertz frequency) to communicate; and the only lasting bond seems to be between female manatees and their calves.

Although aspects of the Amazonian manatee's behavior seem typical of manatees in general, in its remote riverine habitat its existence differs somewhat from that of West Indian and West African manatees. One of the differences concerns feeding habits. Like other manatees, the Amazonian manatee's diet consists primarily of aquatic vascular plants, and captive adult manatees eat between 9 and 15 kilograms (about 20–33 pounds) of vegetation daily. But, in the early 1980s, Robin C. Best made an interesting observation regarding *when* Amazonian manatee may feed. Best noticed that manatees in large lakes or other deep bodies of water in the central Amazon had very little to feed on during the dry season (fall-winter). Water levels can change as much as 10–15 meters (about 30–50 feet) during the annual wet-dry cycle, with the lowest levels in November and December. Best suggested that manatees confined to areas where lowered water levels prevented access to living vegetation in the dry season might consume some dead vegetation, but otherwise the animals fasted. Apparently, the species' very low metabolic rate (only about 36% of the rate that one would expect for a mammal its size), coupled with the accumulation of fat deposits during the wet season, allows the animals to survive a prolonged fast. Best suggested that a fat manatee could survive without eating for up to 200 days on its fat reserves. In fact, not all manatees do survive during extremely dry years, and Amazonian fishermen have reported that, during the dry season, manatees are found dead, apparently due to bowel obstruction caused by ingestion of clay. (Dead manatees recovered in winter near Fort Myers, Florida, have had similar obstructions.)

The extreme wet-dry annual cycle influences the behavior and physiology of the Amazonian manatee in ways other than the extremely low metabolic rate. Manatee reproduction is also affected by the climate. Calves are generally born as the waters start to rise after November–December. Best found that the majority of births occur in February, March, April and May (with some births also taking place in December, January, June and July) as water levels rise and availability of food increases. The synchrony of calving, together with the apparent one-year gestation period, suggests that many mature female manatees enter estrus at approximately the same time of year, and that pregnant female manatees carry an extremely heavy energetic burden during the dry season, at which time their fat reserves must support the metabolic needs of the adult female herself, as well as those of her developing fetus. On the other hand, bearing calves as plant productivity increases means that females can ingest enough vegetation to withstand the metabolic demands of lactation which are greater than those of gestation. Although data are not available regarding growth of wild Amazonian manatee calves, it appears that newborn animals are at least 80 centimeters (about 30 inches) long. Research involving captive calves suggests that they increase their weight an average of about 1 kilogram (2 pounds) per week, and increase their length about 1.4

centimeters (about 1/2 inch) per week. The captive calves consume up to about 6 liters of artificial manatee milk each day, and they are weaned after approximately a year.

The life of an Amazonian manatee, then, is strongly influenced by seasonal climatic changes, at least in Brazil. In June, water levels are highest and the animals tend to be dispersed through lakes, large rivers and tributaries. As water levels start to drop in July–August, the manatees migrate to deep-water lakes or to deep parts of rivers, where they may become concentrated in relatively restricted areas. Animals remaining in rivers may face more energetic demands than those faced by manatees in lakes, because river-dwellers have to expend energy to stay in place against currents. In any event, as the dry season progresses, the manatees occupy deep spots and travel and feed very little until the waters rise again. When food becomes available once more (as water levels start to rise in December) calves are born, mating occurs and the manatees disperse from the deep water areas and start to replenish their exhausted fat reserves. It is important to realize that what is true for manatees in the upper and middle reaches of Amazonia may not hold true for those in other areas.

Surviving a prolonged annual dry-season fast is not the only hazard that the Amazonian manatee faces and that most other manatees apparently do not face. The Florida manatee, at least, has few natural predators, but the Amazonian species apparently is preyed on by jaguars, caimans and sharks. Lack of habitat during the dry season concentrates manatees, and at such times, the animals are particularly susceptible to human predation as well; in fact, dry-season slaughters of manatees concentrated in lakes has been documented. In the remote forests of the Amazon basin, the impact of natural and human predators on the manatee population is difficult to assess.

Even if precise figures were available regarding the number of manatee deaths each year, one problem with assessing the actual impact of mortality on wild populations is that the sizes of those populations are not known. No doubt, most Amazonian manatees inhabit Brazilian waterways. The species is considered rare, if not close to extinction, in Peru and Colombia, and uncommon in most of its range in Eastern Ecuador. Whatever the size of the current population, it is clear that the remainder represents just a fraction of the population that used to exist. Hunting has been the primary culprit, with the greatest exploitation probably occurring between 1935 and 1954, when many tens of thousands of manatee skins were exported from the Amazon, and in the late 1950s when meat harvest peaked. Natural conditions can also contribute to catastrophic mortality; for example, in 1963 (an especially dry year) hundreds of manatees were killed when lakes and rivers dried up in areas such as Tefé, Coari and Manacapuru. It is likely that habitat destruction and hunting pressure are causing the population to decline at a steady but unquantified rate.

Although data exist to document historical levels of harvest of Amazonian manatees, the data base regarding manatee abundance and distribution, life history and habitat requirements is inadequate. In recognition of both the human impact on manatees and the lack of scientific data, the Brazilian government's Instituto Nacional de Pesquisas da Amazonia (INPA) initiated the Projeto Peixe-Boi, the Brazilian Manatee Project, in 1975 (*peixe-boi* means fish ox, the term Brazilians use for manatees). Most of the information available today on Amazonian manatees has resulted from studies done by members of the Projeto Peixe-Boi, centered in Manaus, Brazil. The original goals of the project were to define the distribution and evaluate the status of the species; to study its basic ecology; to develop husbandry techniques for the captive rearing of young and adult animals; and to develop a general conservation plan and the creation of national parks and/or biological preserves to preserve the species in the face of the rapid development taking place in Brazilian Amazonia.

The many members of the project engaged in a variety of studies. The distribution of manatees in Brazil was documented, and food and feeding habits were investigated. Digestibility studies were done for certain plants and for manatee milk. One finding was that the Amazonian manatee can tolerate very low sodium levels in its diet (handy for a freshwater species). Metabolism, respiratory physiology, thermoregulation and cardiac physiology were examined. One observation of these studies was that manatees did not show pronounced bradycardia (slowing of heart rate) during normal dives. The myology (dealing with the muscles) was described, indicating some special adaptations for feeding and swimming. Tooth movement and replacement were measured, showing that the teeth are continuously replaced, that they move anteriorly about one millimeter per month and that tooth movement is probably initiated as calves begin to consume plant material.

In more specific studies, a radio-tagged manatee was tracked for 20 days; it moved about 2.7 kilometers (1.7 miles) per day and was equally active during both night and day. Activity patterns of captive manatees showed that the animals spend about 8 hours per day feeding, 4 hours sleeping and 12 hours moving around. The anatomy and spectral sensitivity of the eye were described, and results of studies indicated that manatees have some binocularity and can produce a well-focused image underwater. Finally, skeletal material and information regarding the impact of local people on manatees were collected.

A large amount of data was collected in a relatively short time, in part because a number of captive manatees were maintained and studied. Physiological research proved particularly fruitful using the captive manatee colony in Manaus. But even though funds were available for the captive animal facility, the Projeto Peixe-Boi was not adequately supported and the scientists had to overcome financial shortages and instability. Tragically, in December 1986,

Robin Best, the leader of the project, died of leukemia, and since his death, studies in the Manaus center have slowed. As indicated in a 1990 publication by F.A.P. Colares and coworkers, studies continue in Manaus using 11 captive manatees (6 female, 5 male) held in two pools.

Although the Projeto Peixe-Boi was a success in providing information about a species for which good data previously did not exist, scientists are still uncertain about a number of aspects of Amazonian manatee biology, including reproductive rates, age-specific mortality rates, longevity, population size, and physical and genetic discreteness of groups of manatees occupying the various waterways of the Amazon basin.

The project was also a success in terms of management and conservation of the Amazonian manatee. Between 1980 and 1984, 42 manatees were introduced into the first hydroelectric reservoir on the Amazon, Curuá-una, near Santarém (Brazil). Although construction of reservoirs is not beneficial to many species, they provide large, stable habitats for manatees. Further, because the colonists around Curuá-una are mainly employed in agriculture, rather than fishing or hunting, the manatees in the reservoir may be relatively safe from predation. The manatees in Curuá-una reservoir were radio tagged, and considerable information has been gathered regarding their behavior, habitat preferences and other aspects of their biology. The project also led to better education of local people and to legislation that in 1986 provided agents of both the Brazilian federal fisheries agency and the federal forestry agency with the authority to protect manatees, as well as other marine mammals.

Research on Amazonian manatees has been most evident in Brazil, but a fairly recent publication (1986) considered the ecology, distribution, harvest and conservation of the species in Ecuador. The authors (Robert M. Timm, Luis Albuja V. and Barbara L. Clausen) describe sightings of manatees in Napo Province, in eastern Ecuador. Although manatees were observed or reported in several locations, the only place where manatees are thought to be abundant (although the term was not quantified) was in the Lagarto Cocha area. As they do elsewhere, the manatees in Ecuador feed mainly on aquatic vascular plants, although they have also been reported to graze on grasses on the edges of sand banks.

In Ecuador, the Siona Indians historically harvested manatees for food, and manatee hunting is a skill that has traditionally been passed from father to son. Today, however, the reduced size of the manatee population has led the Siona voluntarily to ban manatee hunting among themselves to protect the few remaining animals. (Apparently the ban is not absolute, as Thomas O'Shea reported the killing and eating of a manatee by Siona Indians, including a chief, in 1987.) Whether they hunt the animals or not, the Siona continue to be a source of information about manatees.

Other manatee hunters in eastern Ecuador are not so conservation-minded, and the development of the area for oil exploration has brought increased numbers of settlers, as well as an increased military presence. (More military personnel are brought in whenever any conflicts erupt across the Peruvian-Ecuadorian border.) A manatee hunter who lived near the border,

Education efforts and legislation may help protect the Amazonian manatee, or peixe-boi *(fish ox), in Brazil.* Photograph by Alice J. Monroe

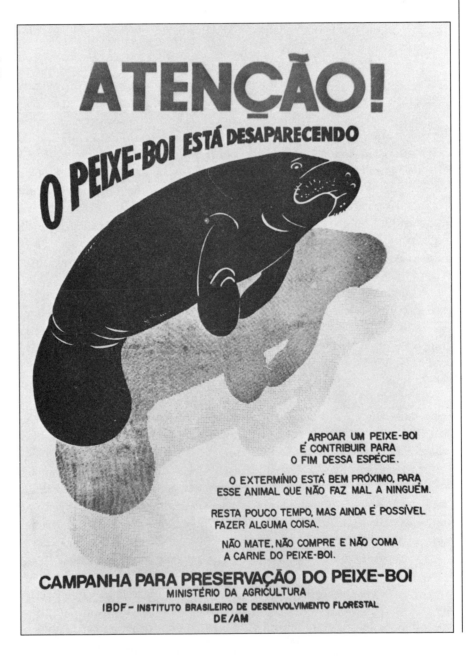

ATENÇÃO!

O PEIXE-BOI ESTÁ DESAPARECENDO

ARPOAR UM PEIXE-BOI É CONTRIBUIR PARA O FIM DESSA ESPÉCIE.

O EXTERMÍNIO ESTÁ BEM PRÓXIMO, PARA ESSE ANIMAL QUE NÃO FAZ MAL A NINGUÉM.

RESTA POUCO TEMPO, MAS AINDA É POSSÍVEL FAZER ALGUMA COISA.

NÃO MATE, NÃO COMPRE E NÃO COMA A CARNE DO PEIXE-BOI.

CAMPANHA PARA PRESERVAÇÃO DO PEIXE-BOI
MINISTÉRIO DA AGRICULTURA
IBDF - INSTITUTO BRASILEIRO DE DESENVOLVIMENTO FLORESTAL
DE/AM

and his two assistants, provided manatee meat to military forces of both Peru and Ecuador. This hunter would silently approach a manatee in a dugout canoe and spear the animal using a 3-meter-long (about 10 feet long) harpoon with a barbed steel tip called an *anzuelo* (fish hook). The manatees were most effectively harvested during the dry season, at dawn or dusk. In one eight-month period, the hunter killed 7–10 manatees, and he claimed to have killed about 100 manatees. The primary limitation on his take was availability of salt to preserve the meat. With adequate salt, his goal would be to take one adult manatee, or two juveniles, daily.

Timm and his colleagues believe that habitat destruction, pollution resulting from oil exploration, hunting pressure to supply meat to the military, subsistence hunting and the low reproductive rate of the manatees make their continued existence in Ecuador questionable. These problems are exacerbated by the remoteness of manatee habitats (making protection difficult) and the international nature of waterways occupied by the manatees. Some local areas are theoretically protected (e.g., the upper Cuyabeno region is part of the Reserva de Producción Faunística Cuyabeno, and the upper Yasuni and Anangu rivers are both within Parque Nacional Yasuni), but enforcement is difficult due to lack of enforcement personnel and to the remoteness of the regions to be patrolled. The scientists concluded that ". . . if the current level of harvest continues unabated, Amazonian manatees will be gone from Ecuadorian waters within 10–15 years."

Despite the success of the Projeto Peixe-Boi and the recent study in Ecuador, research, education, and management efforts need to be extended and enhanced in Amazonia. The habitat destruction and alteration that humans have caused in the Amazon basin have been well documented. The rate of deforestation in Brazil can be exemplified by considering Rondonia, where agricultural development began to expand in the mid-1970s, an area of about 243,000 square kilometers (about 95,000 square miles). In 1975, 1,200 square kilometers (460 square miles) of forest had been cleared for agriculture; in 1982, more than 10,000 square kilometers (4,000 square miles) had been cleared; and in 1985, about 16,000 square kilometers (6,000 square miles) of forest were gone.

Tropical forests, such as that in Rondonia, are complex, diverse biomes that probably contain over half the species on earth, even though they cover only 7% of the land surface on the planet. In fact, tropical rain forests are the most diverse, species- rich biomes on earth. It is tragic that habit degradation and destruction are occurring faster in the world's tropical forests than in any other biome.

As the forests disappear, so do species. In Amazonian Peru, a one-hectare area (about 2.5 acres) of forest can contain as many as 300 species of plants and animals. Forest eradication could lead to the extinction of millions of species, many of which have not ever been classified by scientists. The magnitude and rate of extinction could be greater than in any other time since life began.

The Amazonian manatee could ultimately become extinct, not because of hunting pressure, which the species has faced for millennia, but due to habitat destruction. Elimination of forests causes erosion and increases runoff that can contain pollutants. Deforestation may also lead to large-scale reduction of water levels, which could threaten manatee survival during dry-season fasts. Water and biogeochemical cycles change when the land is denuded of forests, and vegetation available for the manatees will decrease. As with the other sirenians, survival of Amazonian manatees depends on managing human activities.

In essence, the survival of Amazonian manatees depends on maintenance of critical habitat. Is the reverse also true—is the integrity of the aquatic habitat of the Amazon Basin tied to the survival of manatees there? The Amazonian manatee is the largest herbivore in the area. A 200-kilogram (440-pound) manatee may consume 6,000 kilograms (132,000 pounds) of vegetation annually, and return 2,400 kilograms (5,280 pounds) of organic material (in the form of fecal waste) to the environment. The precise role that these large herbivores might have in the Amazon is unknown, but it is obvious that this delicate environment would change without the manatee.

THE
DUGONG

The dugong is remarkable, relative to other sirenians, for a number of reasons. Dugongs have smoother skin than West African and West Indian manatees, a split tail fluke, and tusks. Dugongs are the most marine of the sirenians in their preference of habitat, and they are the only Indo-Pacific sirenians alive today. The dugong is also the most abundant of the sirenian species. And yet the dugong, like its relatives, has been and continues to be affected by humans, both directly for food and other products and indirectly as its habitat is degraded.

A great deal is known about the dugong, due in large part to the efforts of scientists at James Cook University of North Queensland, in Townsville, Australia. A number of individuals, including Helene Marsh, George Heinsohn, Alister Spain, Tony Preen, and Judith Wake have been based in Townsville and have studied the behavior, anatomy, population dynamics and food habits of dugongs, both in Australia and in other parts of the species range. Other scientists, including Paul Anderson and Brydget Hudson, based in Papua New Guinea and Shark Bay on the west coast of Australia have also added to the pool of information regarding dugongs.

ANATOMY

The body of the dugong is spindle-shaped and gray in color. The skin is smooth. Unlike the manatee, the posterior part of the dugong's body is laterally compressed and the tail is in the form of a fluke (like a dolphin's tail) rather than round and spatulate; also, the dugong has no fingernails. Like the manatee, the dugong has hairs scattered over the surface of its body; and tiny external ear openings that are mere pinholes. The valvelike nostrils are situated at the tip of the snout so that only a tiny portion of the animal's head has to be above the surface when it breathes. The dugong's muzzle is distinctly turned downward and ends in a broadly flattened area, called the rostral disk.

Maximum length for the dugong is about 3.3 meters (about 11 feet) but average adult length is about 2.7 meters (about 9 feet). The weight of a 3-meter-long (10-foot-long) animal is about 400 kilograms (880 pounds), and the weight of an average-sized adult is on the order of 250–300 kilograms (550–660 pounds). The largest recorded dugong was a 4.06-meter (13.3-foot), 1,016-kilogram (2,235-pound) specimen, although in light of the existing data on body size, it is likely that a measurement error was made when the specimen was examined. Likewise, a 4.5-meter (14.8-foot) specimen of a Florida manatee was reported, which contrasts markedly with records that cite the longest animal as 3.9 meters (12.8 feet) long.

The dugong's skeleton is similar to that of the manatee in the most general sense. Hind limbs are absent, but vestigial pelvic bones remain embedded in the muscles in the pelvic area, and the bones are extremely dense. Daryl Domning has shown recently that the sex of a dugong can be determined from the shape of the pelvic bones. The skull of the dugong is massive and the rostrum is down-turned, reflecting its bottom feeding habits. The premaxillary bones (at the front of the upper jaw) are greatly enlarged and house the distinctive tusks (incisors) that erupt through the gums in males at puberty (9–10 years of age) but rarely in females. Scientists can estimate age by counting growth layers in the tusks. Each quadrant of the jaws has, over the life of the animal, six molariform teeth (three premolars and three molars). All six teeth never erupt at the same time. The premolars and first molars are lost with age, but the last two molars in each quadrant grow throughout the animal's life. This dental pattern contrasts with that of the manatee in which the molariform teeth are replaced continually in a horizontal (back to front) manner through the animal's life. The digestive tract is quite long, typical of herbivores and generally similar to that of manatees. The large intestine may reach a length of 25 meters (82 feet). Microorganisms that live in the large intestine digest the cellulose in the plant material eaten by the dugong.

A female dugong and her calf. The dugong is distinguished from the manatee by a split tail, called a fluke. Drawing by Leslie Ward

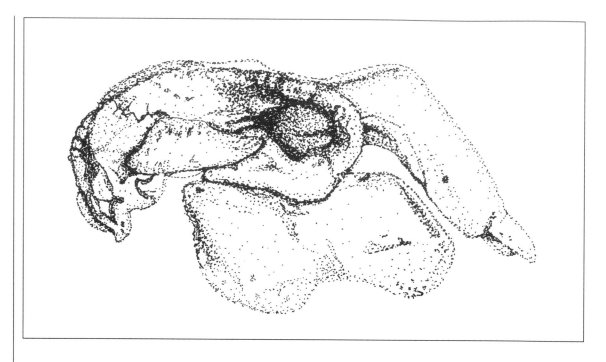

As in the manatees, the lungs of the dugong are long, unlobed and situated dorsally (along the back) in the body cavity. The shape, position and internal structure of the lungs probably help the dugong maintain a horizontal position in the water. Good buoyancy control is also important for bottom feeding. By becoming neutrally buoyant while feeding on the bottom, the dugong does not have to expend energy to stay down. This feat has not been demonstrated scientifically, but is probably accomplished by relaxing or contracting the muscles in the diaphragm and rib cage to change the effective volume of the lungs. The kidneys of the dugong are cylindrical compared with the "lobulated" kidneys in manatees. The Steller's sea cow apparently had kidneys similar in shape to those of cetaceans (whales and dolphins) and pinnipeds (seals). The dugong brain, like that of the manatee, is relatively small for the size of the animal and "smooth," that is, the cerebral cortex is not highly folded like that of primates or cetaceans.

Dugong physiology is not well-known, but probably parallels that of the manatee in many ways. Data suggest that dugongs, like the Florida manatee, are sensitive to environmental temperatures at the southern extremes of their range in Australia and may make local movements to deeper water, where the temperature is more stable. Other aspects of dugong physiology such as diving and sensory capabilities have not been studied. An interesting area of metabolic physiology is water balance. For the most part, dugongs are strictly saltwater animals (compared with manatees which are either strictly freshwater

Skull of the dugong, Dugong dugon. Drawing by Leslie Ward

(Amazonian manatee) or move between freshwater and saltwater (West Indian and West African manatees)) but they are occasionally found in river mouths. Manatees may well require freshwater for drinking, but what about the dugong? The kidney of the dugong is very different from that of the manatee, and one might suspect that, based on habitat (i.e., saltwater), it may be able to produce a urine concentrated enough to eliminate the salt taken in with its food.

DISTRIBUTION

The dugong is widely distributed in the waters of 43 countries along the western Pacific and Indian oceans. The distribution is by no means uniform. This pattern is similar to that seen in the several species of manatees and probably reflects both the unevenness of the distribution of dugong habitat and the impact of humans, particularly in areas where the population is (was) low. Certainly humans have influenced dugong distribution over time. As

Range of the dugong. Drawing by Leslie Ward

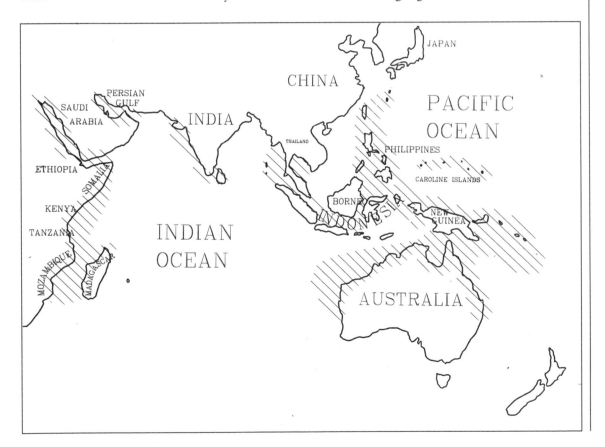

Masaharu Nishiwaki and Helene Marsh have stated "The precise extent to which the dugong's range has been contracted is unknown, but over much of its present range it is now represented by relict populations separated by large areas where it is close to extinction or extinct." Much of the information which follows comes from Nishiwaki and Marsh's 1985 overview of the status of the dugong.

East Africa

The dugong's range in Africa has been reported to extend from Durban, South Africa (where a dugong washed ashore in 1966), into the Red Sea, but it is likely that the southern extent of the range is in Mozambique. The distribution of dugongs in East Africa is not continuous. In most locations, dugongs are scarce, although there is a report of a herd of several hundred off the south coast of Somalia. Recent surveys have reported a few dugongs around Antonio Eres in northern Mozambique, in Kenya, and near reefs at Ile Sainte-Marie, east-central Madagascar. Dugongs are protected in the Paradise Islands National Park in Mozambique. According to Pieter Folkens' 1989 letter to *Sirenews*, the Malagasy name for the dugong is *lambondana*, which means "wild pig of the coral."

Historically, dugongs were extremely common around Madagascar and nearby islands. Explorers in the 17th to 19th centuries harvested the animals in large numbers; in fact, one report states "herds of 300–400 animals were sometimes hauled out and shot."

Recent surveys (within the past 10–20 years) of dugongs in East Africa are lacking for most areas. Locations said to have supported dugong populations in the past (and maybe today) include the Pema-Zanzibar Channel and the Rufigi-Mafia Islands of Tanzania; the Kiunga Archipelago and Lamu Inland Sea off the coasts of Kenya and Somalia; Kipini and Malindi, Kenya; and Ras Bur Gao and the archipelago to Kisimayu in Somalia.

Red Sea

Egypt, Ethiopia and Saudi Arabia are the largest countries along the Red Sea, where dugongs have been considered rare. In 1980, a group of 30 dugongs was observed during an aerial survey of inshore waters of the Republic of Djibouti; this was reported as the largest herd ever recorded from the Red Sea and the Gulf of Aden. Anthony Preen subsequently conducted aerial surveys of the area in 1987 and found that dugongs were not as scarce as expected; he estimated that about 800 dugongs exist there.

Persian Gulf

Until the early 1980s dugongs were considered to be rare to extinct in the Persian Gulf. Thirty-eight dugongs, along with many other marine animals, were found dead after the Nowruz oil spill in 1983. It is not known if the oil contributed to the deaths of the dugongs. At the time of the spill, scientists were uncertain whether 38 animals represented a significant portion of the area's dugong population. Subsequent aerial surveys conducted in the Persian Gulf in 1986 by Tony Preen for the Saudi Arabian Meteorology and Environmental Protection Administration found a large herd of approximately 600 dugongs. The surveys by Preen resulted in a population estimate of about 6,500 dugongs. These animals probably use the waters of Saudi Arabia, United Arab Emirates, Bahrain and Qatar. Dugongs have been hunted in the area for centuries as evidenced by 4,000-year-old dugong bones at an archaeological site in Abu Dhabi, United Arab Emirates. Dugong meat is sold at markets in the Arabian Gulf, but, at least in Abu Dhabi and Manama (Bahrain), the dugongs appear to have been caught incidentally to fishing efforts, rather than deliberately harvested.

The military activities in the Gulf in early 1991, including mine clearing, ship sinkings and oil spills, have created additional hazards for the dugongs and other marine life. The full effect of the large oil spill had not been fully assessed, although dugongs have been reported in the oily waters. The hypothermia (an unintentional fall in the body temperature to dangerous levels due to exposure to cold) that sea otters in Alaska experienced following the *Exxon Valdez* spill would not occur in the sirenians, since they do not depend on fur for insulation. The effects of oil are more likely to occur in the respiratory system, due to inhalation of vapors, or in the digestive system, due to ingestion of oil-covered vegetation. Ingestion could either kill dugongs outright or have a debilitating side effect if oil killed the microorganisms in the digestive system responsible for cellulose breakdown and nutrition of the host sirenian.

Asia

As elsewhere, dugong distribution is discontinuous in Asian waters. Much of the information about dugongs is dated. The northern limit of dugong distribution is around Okinawa in the Ryukyu Islands, where the species is rare. Dugongs have not been reported near Japan proper or Korea, although they do exist in undetermined numbers in certain coastal regions of China and Taiwan. Up to 20 dugongs have been reported around Hepu County (China), and incidental catch records exist in Hepu County and elsewhere.

Dugongs are also reported in small numbers from various locations in Indonesia, including bays, reefs and straits around Sulawesi and in West Irian. They are most abundant in the Aru Islands, where fishermen sell dugong tears as an aphrodisiac, and the ends of the tusks as cigarette holders. Although dugongs are apparently abundant in the Aru Islands, a 1979 report indicated that about 1,000 dugongs annually are incidentally caught in shark nets.

Dugongs are also harpooned for their meat, but it appears that shark netting constitutes the greatest threat to dugong survival in the Aru Islands. The April 1984 issue of *Sirenews* reported that the meat of an adult dugong fetches $33, about half the average annual income for a fisherman, and the tusks bring twice that amount. A cotton swab used to dab dugong tears costs about $1, and brings "good luck, prosperity, and success with women."

In the Philippines, dugongs occur in small numbers in parts of Luzon, Palawan, Panay, the Sulu Archipelago, Masbete Island, Cataduanes Island and in the provinces of Camarines Norte. Dugong meat is sold in some markets in the Philippines. Dugongs are also found in eastern and western Malaysia, Thailand and Burma. There appears to be no resident population of dugongs in Bangladesh, although animals may occasionally wander there from Burma. Dugongs are present in undetermined numbers in the Andaman and Nicobar Islands.

The dugong population of India and Sri Lanka is apparently decreasing. Dugongs may be found in the Gulf of Mannar and Palk Bay, located between India and Sri Lanka, and in the Gulf of Cutch in northwestern India. Animals from the latter area may roam into waters off Pakistan. Nishiwaki and Marsh indicate that dugongs are rare along the west coast of India and may be absent from much of the east coast. Fishing activities have apparently been at least a major contributor to the reduction in dugong numbers in India and Sri Lanka. Marsh has reported to *Sirenews* that between April 1983 and August 1984, for example, 250 dugongs were illegally caught and butchered at two villages in southern India.

In a 1989 publication, Stephen Leatherwood and Randall Reeves noted that "direct hunting and netting for meat, incidental catching in shark and turtle nets, habitat degradation caused by extensive trawling for prawns, [and] the widespread use of powered vessels and fishing with dynamite" all affected dugongs in the Gulf of Mannar and Palk Bay. The authors concluded that "few if any dugongs were present in the species' prime areas of past occurrence in Sri Lankan waters." Clearly, intensive conservation efforts, including creation of sanctuaries, are necessary to protect dugongs in India and Sri Lanka.

Micronesia

The only recent information on dugongs comes from the Island of Palau where the population may be just a few tens of animals. In Palau dugong meat is an esteemed food, and the cultural significance of dugongs is great. Nonetheless, continued take of dugongs from the small population in waters of Palau places the animals in serious danger of extinction. Modern technology, including motor boats and spear guns, has increased the effectiveness with which people have impacted dugongs in Palau.

Melanesia

Most of the recent studies of dugongs in Melanesia have occurred in Papua New Guinea and nearby islands, including West New Britain, Manus Island, New Caladonia and Vanuatu. Except along the Papua New Guinea coast (where a 1976 survey accounted for almost 200 animals), dugongs are not common. In the Torres Strait, located between New Guinea and Australia, there may be over 12,000 dugongs, although islanders in the strait are permitted to harvest them. Two Wildlife Management Areas have been established to protect dugongs in Papua New Guinea.

Australia

Most dugong studies have been conducted in Australia, so the distribution and abundance of the species in that country is better understood than in many other parts of the species' range. Much of the information on this species in this volume comes from Australian researchers. Dugongs occur in the northern half of Australia, with the southern limits being Perth on the west coast and extreme southern Queensland on the east coast. In a number of locations, over 100 dugongs have been reported in single aerial surveys; these locations include Moreton Bay, Great Sandy Strait–Hervey Bay–Tin Can Inlet, Shoalwater Bay–Pt. Clinton, Cape Flattery–Cape Melville, Torres Strait, Weipa–Staaten Island, and Wellesley Islands (all on the east coast of Australia), and Exmouth Gulf and Shark Bay (on the west coast). Dugongs are also common in the Gulf of Carpentaria in northern Australia; in the western half of the gulf, a year-round population of about 17,000 dugongs may exist.

Although precise population estimates are not available, Australia is clearly the location where the majority of the world's dugongs live. Marsh recently suggested that the dugong population may number up to 70,000 individuals in Australian waters. They receive protection in that country, although native hunters are allowed to take dugongs in certain areas, and there is incidental take in fishing gear or shark nets placed to protect swimmers at beaches.

The development of a method to estimate the age of dugongs using growth layers in the tusks was a key factor in assessing dugong populations. Maximum estimated age is 73 years. Both males and females become sexually mature at about 10 years of age, but this varies with the individual and some females may not mature until 15 years of age. Dugong reproductive biology seems to be generally similar to what we know about the Florida manatee. Dugongs have an estimated gestation period of 13–14 months. Calving interval is variable and may range from three to seven years. The potential for population growth is about 5% per year. Breeding/calving appear to occur on a year-round basis in tropical areas where dugongs have been studied the most.

However, there seem to be seasonal peaks in reproductive activity. Helene Marsh described male dugong sexual activity (sperm production) patterns as "asynchronous" and "discontinuous." That is, not all sexually mature males are active at the same time and there are periods when none is active. The greatest numbers of males are active when the females are reproductively active.

As with the manatees, human activity is the most significant non-natural mortality factor for dugongs. In addition to hunting, dugongs have been accidentally killed in gill nets and shark nets set to protect swimmers. Natural mortality factors include storm surges from cyclones, parasites, and predation by sharks and killer whales. Diseases of dugongs have not been well studied, but include diseases of the skin, pancreas and gastrointestinal tract.

BEHAVIOR

Although the behavior of the dugong in its natural habitat is difficult to study, recent use of aerial surveys and radio/satellite telemetry is adding rapidly to our information on dugong behavior. Seasonal movements can be inferred from aerial survey data and satellite telemetry has the advantage of allowing 24-hour-per-day tracking without requiring an extensive field team. Diving habits can also be inferred by calculating water depth. If there are seagrasses in the area, one can assume that the dugongs are diving to the bottom to feed. Dugongs are generally considered shallow-water animals and feed in waters just a few meters deep. Dugongs recently observed diving in waters 11–12 meters (36–40 feet) deep suggest that the animals may be at or near their physiological limits. Deeper dives require more surface time to replenish oxygen supplies, and some depth diving becomes inefficient because more energy is used in diving than is gained from the food eaten. Dive times of one male dugong studied by Helene Marsh and Galen Rathbun averaged 1.2–1.5 minutes and ranged from 0.5 to 3.75 minutes. Maximum dive time for the dugong is about 8 minutes.

Positions determined via satellites allow researchers to document individual movement patterns and habitat-use patterns. For example, Marsh and Rathbun have shown that some dugongs spend 95% of their time in ranges of 4 to 11 square kilometers (1.5 to 4.5 square miles). Recent data have shown that one dugong traveled 140 kilometers (87 miles) straight-line in 51 hours (an average speed of about 3 kilometers, or 2 miles, per hour). Attachment of time-depth recording gear to the satellite transmitter will provide quantitative data on dive depths, surface intervals and diurnal patterns of diving.

Dugongs feed strictly on submerged (bottom) vegetation and, although the males have erupted tusks, the tusks are apparently not used for feeding. Dugongs feed on the leaves, roots and rhizomes of seagrasses and dugong "feeding trails" can be seen when seagrass beds are exposed at low tide. Dugongs, like manatees, also ingest invertebrates found in and on the seagrasses, but we do not know if they have any significance in dugong nutrition. Normal feeding patterns appear to be diurnal (during daylight hours) but Helene Marsh has found some evidence that disturbance from boating activities may cause dugongs to feed at night. The same type of switch from diurnal to nocturnal behavior has been documented for the Florida manatee in areas of heavy boat traffic.

The social behavior of wild dugongs is, as one might imagine, difficult to study for logistic reasons. Dugongs often form large herds of several hundred animals but the function of these herds is unclear. Comparisons could be drawn with herds of terrestrial ungulates. It is likely that the female and her calf are the core of the social group, as in the manatee. Lactation may last for 18 months and the weaned calf, although nutritionally independent, may stay with its mother for several years until the next calf is born. The sensory biology of sirenians is largely unknown but sound and vision probably play an important role in establishing and maintaining the bond between female and calf. Calving has only been observed on a few occasions and in all cases the female was in shallow water. In several instances the female was actually aground, but not completely out of the water, until the tide rose.

Dugongs produce low frequency vocalizations, variously described as whistles or bleats, in the 1–8 kilohertz range. Vocalization may be particularly important in female-calf bonding.

The state of our knowledge of dugong social behavior is advancing day by day. Reproductive behavior is always of great interest and one wonders how males manage to locate estrous females. Studies in the Shark Bay area of Australia, where the water is clear enough to make observations from boats or from underwater, suggest that males may establish territories from which they make displays to attract reproductively active females. Infrasound (sound below the level of human hearing capabilities) has been shown to be important in elephant social behavior and is used by estrous females to attract males. Given the long distance that sound, particularly low frequency sound, travels in water, dugongs and manatees in estrous may also use it to attract mates.

Regardless of how the males find the females, the general pattern of mating behavior seems to be similar to that of the manatee: a single estrous female is pursued by several males that compete to mate with her. Tony Preen has described dugong mating behavior as consisting of several "phases." There is a "following" phase in which groups of up to 20 animals move in a tight cluster with a rather erratic path. The group seems to be centered around a single estrous female. The next phase may be the "fighting" phase, consisting of violent activity including splashing, tail thrashing, rolls and body lunges. This appears to be much more violent than manatee mating behavior. The "fighting" phase appears to precede the "mounting" phase in which one male mounts the female from beneath while several others may cling to them. It is not clear if one or more males successfully mate with the female. Preen described the animals as being exhausted after these violent bouts of activity. The descriptions of dugong mating behavior are few and seem to vary with geographic location and among observers. As with most aspects of dugong biology, much remains to be learned.

STELLER'S
SEA COW:
A STORY
OF HUMAN
NEGLIGENCE

Steller's sea cow (*Hydrodamalis gigas*) is unique among sirenians for a variety of reasons. The species was among the largest known sirenians, reaching a length of perhaps 8 meters (26 feet). It occupied cold, subarctic waters, rather than the tropical or subtropical waters inhabited by most sirenians (including all species now living); it lacked teeth, finger bones and apparently the ability to dive; and it is the only sirenian species whose extinction is attributed to human activities. The extinction process itself was remarkable, occurring as it did within 27 years after the species was discovered by Russian explorers.

The sea cow was discovered in November 1741 when the Russian brig *Saint Peter* became wrecked on an uninhabited island near the remote Aleutian chain off Alaska. The island, and indeed the entire sea around the island, were later named in honor of Vitus Bering, the captain of the brig. Although Bering died and was buried on the island, most of his crew survived, in part because food on Bering Island was abundant. A primary source of that food was one that was new to the men—the meat of a huge, unknown marine mammal.

The crew of the *Saint Peter* could hardly have been in worse shape when they arrived on Bering Island. Demoralized and plagued with scurvy, their fate seemed sealed when they found themselves stranded on an unknown island at the onset of the Arctic winter. The presence of the gigantic sea cows must have seemed too good to be true. The animals were abundant in the shallow waters off the island, and they showed no fear as they floated at the surface, resting or chewing their food, a brown alga called kelp. Hunters hooked the animals, and several men could drag the carcass ashore for butchering. The adult sea cows weighed 4 metric tons or more, so one kill meant lots of meat, and to the delight of the men, the meat and fat proved delicious. The meat was said to resemble beef, and the fat smelled and tasted something like almond oil.

By summer 1742, the crew had used parts of the *Saint Peter* to build a small boat to take them home. Following their return to Kamchatka (Russia) in 1742, the survivors of the winter on Bering Island told others of the wealth of furs and other products to be had in the Bering Sea and Alaska. They also told of the immense sea cows that could be taken for food with so little effort. Subsequent voyages by explorers and hunters began to schedule stops on Bering Island or nearby Copper Island to stock up on sea cow meat, while exploiting the furbearers living on the islands. The naturalist Leonard Stejneger wrote in 1887 that as early as 1743, crews wintered on Bering Island, and "until 1763 hardly a winter passed without one or more parties spending eight or nine months in hunting fur-animals there, during which time the crews lived almost exclusively on the meat of the sea-cow." As many as 130 men may have wintered on Bering Island annually. Although the fur hunters on Bering and Copper Islands harvested many sea cows, they were not the only people who craved sea cow meat. Stejneger revealed that many vessels

Russian hunters kill a Steller's sea cow for food while arctic foxes wait for scraps. Due to wholesale slaughter, the species became extinct 27 years after its discovery. Painting by Alfred J. Milotte

heading east from Russia toward Alaska stopped to "lay in stores of sea-cow meat" to support their two to three year voyages.

The harvest of sea cows, especially by some of the overwintering fur hunters, was extremely wasteful. The method of hunting involved single hunters (rather than teams) who secured sea cows by sneaking up on them in shallow water and spearing them with iron-shod poles. The mortally wounded animals reacted to this violent attack by swimming offshore, where they died. If a carcass washed ashore soon after death, the hunters butchered it and consumed the meat; however, if the carcass either washed ashore after some decomposition had occurred or drifted out to sea, the meat was wasted. Even greater waste is alleged. One source contended that some crews ate only the kidneys of the sea cow, with the rest of the carcass being left for the Arctic foxes and other scavengers (though other sources indicated that all the meat of harvested sea cows was consumed by the hunters).

A mining engineer named Jakovleff, sent to Copper Island by the Russian government to investigate copper resources there, commented that the island, first visited by the Russians in 1745, had no more sea cows by 1754; therefore, he and his party were forced to stay on Bering Island where sea cow meat was available. There, he observed the wasteful slaughter of sea cows and predicted that the species would disappear from Bering Island as it had around Copper Island, if appropriate steps were not taken. Stejneger examined harvest records and log books of early explorers and fur hunters and estimated that, when the sea cow was discovered, only about 2,000 of the animals existed. Jakovleff formally petitioned authorities to stop the wasteful manner by which the fur hunters harvested sea cows; his petition, filed in 1755, was ignored. The sea cows were gone only 13 years later. Given the small size of the sea cow population, the intense hunting pressure the population suffered, as well as the wasteful manner of harvest, there is little wonder that extinction occurred so quickly.

Considering man's brief exposure to Steller's sea cow, it is remarkable that we know as much as we do about this unusual creature. The source of most of the available scientific information is the naturalist Georg Wilhelm Steller, who was a member of Bering's shipwrecked crew.

Steller spent the winter of 1741 on Bering Island with the other survivors of the wreck of the *Saint Peter*. He busied himself by collecting and recording detailed observations of the plants, animals and minerals he found on the island and by caring for sick members of the crew. Steller left Bering Island with the crew in the summer of 1742 with just a few biological specimens and his notes. After arriving in Kamchatka, Steller made arrangements for his notes to be printed, but he died, at age 37, before publication occurred. As the well-known marine mammal scientist Victor Scheffer has remarked, "all that is known of the sea cow is contained in posthumous literature—edited, copied and translated without the help of the one man who knew the animal best."

Steller's notes, together with studies of bones found on Bering and Copper Islands, comprise the majority of information regarding the sea cow. Descriptions of the species' anatomy help scientists conjecture about how it could survive in a harsh environment that contrasts so strongly with the environment of living sirenians.

In terms of its external appearance, the sea cow had a small head (about one-tenth of the total body length), a short neck, a split tail fluke (somewhat similar to that of the dugong, and very different from the rounded tail of manatees), and short, stubby pectoral flippers. The rough, barklike epidermis was reported to be so tough that even an axe had difficulty cutting it. The sea cow's maximum length has been documented at about 8 meters (26 feet), but the maximum weight is uncertain. Steller's own notes were widely inconsistent in terms of sea cow weight; at one point the weight was given as 8,000 pounds (80 hundredweight) and elsewhere the weight was reported to be about 48,000 pounds (480 long hundredweight). Using models, Victor Scheffer calculated a maximum weight of 10 metric tons, but others have placed the probable weight closer to 4 metric tons.

Internally, the sea cow had a number of interesting traits. Steller compared the sea cow flipper with an amputated limb, and commented that the most unusual feature of the sea cow was its limb structure. The bones in the forearm were blunt and thick and the flippers lacked individual finger bones. The skull was also unusual, relative to that of other sirenians, because it lacked teeth. Instead, "horny plates" in the front of its mouth helped the animal crush its food (soft plants). Unlike that of some sirenians, the front of the skull (the rostrum) was not very strongly curved down. The internal organs appeared unusual to Steller, who had never examined another sirenian; actually the large lungs, specialized digestive tract, and other features resembled those of other sirenians.

The unusual adaptations of the sea cow make sense when one examines the sea cow's environment, as described by paleontologist Daryl Domning. About the time Steller's sea cows evolved, the waters of the North Pacific cooled a great deal. In this cooler environment, kelps (large brown algae) rather than seagrasses predominated. To survive on kelp, the sea cows had to become adapted to the cooler temperatures, to the turbulent, inshore conditions where kelps flourish and occasionally, to being smashed into rocks by waves. Adaptations favoring survival under such circumstances would include a large body size to help conserve heat and a thick skin both for insulation and for protection when encountering rocky outcrops. These adaptations caused the skeleton to represent a smaller percentage of the sea cow's body weight, leading to greater buoyancy. The buoyancy, in turn, was advantageous for a number of reasons. Kelp is available at the surface, and while the sea cows basked with their dark-skinned backs exposed, they were able to absorb heat from the sun. Floating high in the water also allowed the sea cows to enter shallow areas where they could feed or escape from predators (such as killer whales) less able to enter such areas. Seabirds could pick parasites from the

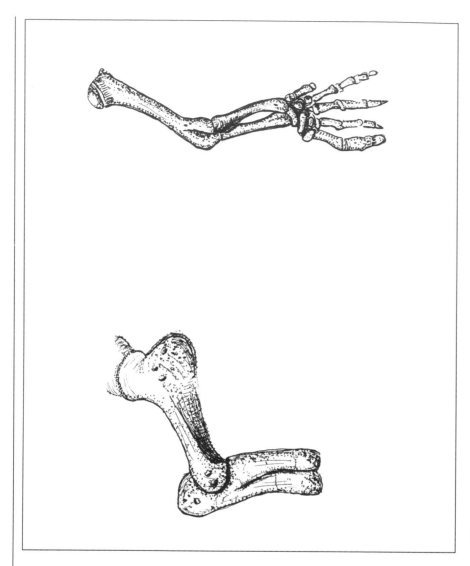

The pectoral limbs of two sirenians. The West African manatee's limb (top) has a full complement of limb bones, including "wrist" and "finger" bones. Steller's sea cow lacked the distal bones, having only a humerus, radius and ulna. Drawing by Leslie Ward

skin of floating sea cows, and as a result, wave drag on swimming sea cows may have been reduced. Domning also explains that entry into shallow areas had some hazards induced by strong currents or waves. The animals compensated by swimming slowly into the current as they grazed, using their flexible neck to reach out to feed. When in danger of colliding with rocks, the clawlike flippers could push off the bottom or pull against wave surges.

Such theories provide some insight into how sea cows lived successfully in such a harsh environment. Apparently, the species frequented shallow, sandy, nearshore areas, especially near river mouths. The animals came particularly close to shore during high tide. The sea cows were observed in small groups, said to be family groups, that ate almost constantly. (The same anthropomorphic interpretation of "family" group was later applied to manatees but turned out to be false; father manatees do none of the rearing or care of young.) While eating, the sea cows appeared oblivious to their surroundings, including human predators.

To feed, the sea cows used either their lips or flippers to gather and push food into the mouth. Although they consumed just the leafy parts of plants, the animals uprooted lots of vegetation as they grazed. Grazing occupied much of the sea cows' time in summer, and the animals became quite rotund. In winter, little food was available, and as a consequence, their appearance changed dramatically: Their ribs showed clearly through their thick skin, and a pronounced hollow area existed along the backbone. When they were not feeding, the sea cows traveled slowly, using their tail flukes for locomotion. The only time that the flippers were used much was to push the sea cow away from rocks when waves were strong.

The social and reproductive behavior of the sea cow, as interpreted by Steller, sounds quite chivalrous. That interpretation is likely to be untrue. The sea cows were said to be monogamous. They mated in the spring, especially during the evening hours, following extensive and elaborate courtship. Most calves were seen in autumn. The adults showed some measure of protective behavior for their young by shielding the calves from rocky shorelines and intruders. In fact, epimeletic (care-giving) behavior occurred among sea cows

The skull of a Steller's sea cow, Hydrodamalis gigas. Drawing by Leslie Ward

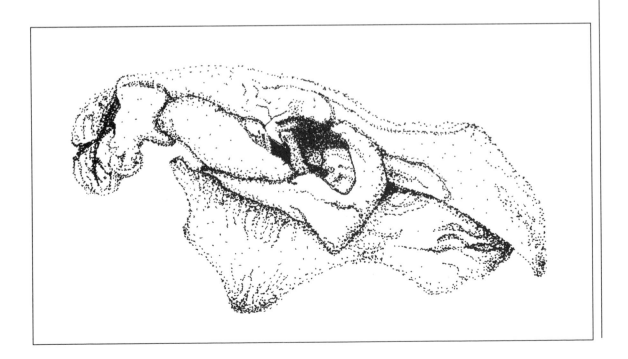

of all sizes; when, for example, an animal was harpooned, other animals stayed with the victim, sometimes following it onto the shore.

Romantics still maintain that Steller's sea cow lives, much as Kipling wrote in "The White Seal," in some isolated haunt where humans cannot locate them. Publications as late as 1884 asserted that individual sea cows survived until the mid-1800s. But the truth, as Leonard Stejneger argued in 1887, is that Steller's sea cow became extinct by 1768. Stejneger's conclusion is brief and direct: "It was simply due to man's greed, and he accomplished it within the short time of twenty-seven years."

Slow breeding, small population size and limited range contributed to the sea cow's demise. These characteristics apply today to many marine mammals that are killed, deliberately or incidentally, by humans. The little vaquita, or Gulf of California harbor porpoise (*Phocoena sinus*), is found only in upper parts of the Gulf of California, where it may number just a few hundred individuals; but fishing gear kills tens of vaquitas annually. The baiji

Steller's sea cow occupied a cold environment, unlike living sirenians, and subsisted on kelp. Drawing by Leslie Ward

or Yangtze River dolphin (*Lipotes vexillifer*) is endemic to that river and may be the most endangered cetacean, with less than 400 individuals left. The Hawaiian monk seal (*Monachus schauinslandi*), of which about 1,000 or fewer remain, is affected by a variety of human activities. And, of course, sirenians, including the Florida manatee and the Amazonian manatee, geographically restricted and rare, are killed by people.

Sirenians and many other marine mammals are very susceptible to extinction. And, as with the giant sea cow, depletion can occur so quickly that science and management cannot react in time. The negligence and greed that led to the sea cow's extinction should serve as an example so that people intent on short-term gains do not wipe out other, similarly vulnerable species.

CONSERVATION

In its annual report to Congress for 1989, the Marine Mammal Commission stated that the manatee is one of the most endangered marine mammals in U.S. waters. As we have seen, the other sirenians also face the threats of habitat loss, hunting and other perils associated with humans. Strong conservation efforts are needed to save these species from extinction.

In a paper entitled "New Principles for the Conservation of Wild Living Resources," Sidney J. Holt and Lee M. Talbot noted that the term "conservation" has been used to mean many things. The authors stated that some of the goals of a conservation program should include wise use of a resource and keeping that resource for future use. "In its broad definition, it [conservation] includes management measures, and means the collection and application of biological information for the purposes of increasing and maintaining the number of animals within species and populations at some optimum level with respect to their habitat. Used in this way, conservation refers to the entire scope of activities that constitute a modern scientific resource program, including research, census, law enforcement, habitat acquisition and improvement, and periodic or total protection as well as regulated taking."

Holt and Talbot list four general principles of conservation programs, which include the following: maintaining the ecosystem in a desirable state; including safety factors in management decisions "to allow for the facts that knowledge is limited and institutions are imperfect"; formulating and applying conservation measures for a resource in ways that do not waste other resources; and ensuring that "monitoring, analysis, and assessment precede planned use and accompany actual use of wild living resources." The definitions and principles outlined by Holt and Talbot apply well to conservation programs for sirenians around the world.

Manatees in Florida are protected by two major pieces of federal legislation (the Marine Mammal Protection Act of 1972 and the Endangered Species Act of 1973), as well as the Florida Manatee Sanctuary Act of 1978. The federal laws prohibit such activities as killing, injuring, capturing, harassing (defined as changing the "normal" behavior of an animal) or attempting any such activities, with penalties of up to $20,000 and/or a year in prison for violations. Even chasing and handling a manatee is illegal. The Florida legislation is the most recent in a series of state acts designed to protect manatees (the first was in 1893); the 1978 legislation established the state of Florida as a manatee refuge and sanctuary and created boat-speed regulatory zones in locations where manatees are likely to be abundant. Thus, there is no lack of a legal framework for protecting the species. Fortunately, there is already considerable coordination of effort among the various state and federal agencies, private organizations and individuals who work with the species. Some key organizations and agencies involved in conservation are the Marine Mammal Commission and the U.S. Fish and Wildlife Service (federal government), the Florida Department of Natural Resources and the Florida Game and Freshwater Fish Commission (state government), Florida Power & Light Company and the Save the Manatee Club with 20,000 members around the United States. (A list of some of these organizations appears at the back of this volume.) The effective interaction of these and other groups and individuals is important, but there are many areas in which continued effort is necessary and in which improvements, including research, habitat protection, planning and permitting, law enforcement and education, would lead to enhanced manatee protection.

Without adequate and up-to-date scientific data regarding manatees and their habitat, efforts to manage and conserve manatees will not be as effective as they could be. For example, how can managers protect critical manatee habitat if scientists have not determined the characteristics and locations of that habitat? Without data on where and how manatees die, rational, effective steps can not be taken to reduce or eliminate that mortality. Although scientific research on manatees has taught us a great deal about the species and its needs, continued and expanded research efforts must include further carcass salvage, radio and satellite telemetry and continued study of manatee use of coastal habitats, population dynamics and certain physiological characteristics.

Habitat conservation is another area where considerable work is needed, if manatees are to survive in Florida for future generations to enjoy. A number of scientists have noted that conservation efforts directed at a particular species must go hand-in-hand with efforts to protect the habitat necessary for survival and proliferation of that species. It is also apparent that the only way to assess which habitats are most important to a species is to perform laborious field research on the ecology of that species. Noted ecologist Daniel Simberloff of Florida State University states that "if one really wants to conserve species, such research is the only guarantor of success."

Imagine trying to conserve manatees in Florida and at the same time permitting coastal development to run rampant. Eliminating the food sources of manatees would destroy the species just as effectively as direct killing by watercraft, hunters or disease. And yet loss of habitat for manatees and other coastal species has occurred at an alarming rate in Florida. In a relatively undeveloped area of the Florida coast, Charlotte Harbor, a 1986 report indicated that wetlands have declined by 23% from their original extent, seagrasses by 22%, salt marshes by 51%, mudflats by 75% and oyster reefs by 39%. Dredge-and-fill operations have eliminated 81% of the seagrasses and 44% of the mangroves and tidal marshes in Tampa Bay. These examples demonstrate that the inshore environment of Florida has been greatly altered, mostly by human activities. The manatee is not the only endangered species— the manatee's situation is only one symptom of a crisis (poorly controlled human activities and growth) that is devastating fisheries, seagrasses and other vital components of Florida's inshore environment. To underscore this interpretation, some scientists believe that habitat loss is the most critical fish and wildlife problem in the United States today.

Several approaches, employed jointly, would help conserve critical manatee habitat. The first step is for the federal and state governments to acquire shoreline property and create a system of sanctuaries and refuges, where human activities would be prohibited, or at least minimized. Manatees have learned to use the few sanctuaries that exist, so a system of such refuges, containing critical resources such as vegetation for food, freshwater for drinking and sources of warm water in winter, would provide safe havens for manatees. Setting aside such areas is a step that would help conserve manatees and other natural resources, but such acquisition must occur soon, before large tracts of undeveloped waterfront land either become developed or prohibitively expensive. Although both the federal and state governments have acquired critical manatee habitat (as has a private organization, The Nature Conservancy), further efforts are needed to assure adequate manatee habitat in the future.

Two other ways that habitat protection could occur are via restrictions on human activities (including building marinas or other boating facilities) in critical manatee areas and use of mitigation banking, which involves habitat protection that compensates for unavoidable, necessary habitat losses associated with future development projects. For example, mitigation banking might require developers who destroy habitat in one location to restore or protect critical habitat elsewhere.

Another important factor in conservation is planning for population growth. In Florida, 90% of the human population occupies areas within 10 miles of the coast. That population is growing by at least 800–1,000 new residents each day. The incredible growth of the human population of Florida, along with the activities of that population, have caused deterioration of the freshwater supply, water and air quality, and living natural resources. A report by the Florida Department of Community Affairs points out that the state's lack of a balanced growth plan has threatened "air, water, beaches, wetlands, and other natural resources . . . essential to lasting prosperity."

Despite the gloomy, long-term view of environmental quality in Florida, there is still a strong tendency among some to consider the short term and continue the development trend that has placed the state's natural resources in such a precarious position. To address the shortcomings in past plans that were designed to address human population growth, the Florida legislature passed the Local Government Comprehensive Planning and Land Regulation Act in 1985. The Act requires counties and municipalities to develop long-range plans for handling human population growth in ways that also consider maintenance or improvement of water quality, wildlife habitat and endangered species. Good, comprehensive local plans, which must be completed no later than 1991, must take into account the biology and ecology of manatees, as well as manatee critical habitat. Planners with the Florida Department of Natural Resources have worked and continue to work vigorously with local governments to assure that manatees are adequately considered in local management plans.

The Department of Natural Resources has also worked to promote passage of legislation at the statewide level to protect manatees and manatee habitat. Recent legislation signed by Florida Governor Martinez and which became effective July 1, 1990, provided the Department of Natural Resources with additional funding and authority to protect manatees and their habitat. Although this legislation has many valuable components that should greatly facilitate conservation of manatees, two especially important components restrict construction of powerboat slips and regulate boat speeds in certain counties where manatees occur frequently and/or where watercraft-related manatee mortality is very high.

The federal government also regulates human activities through enforcement of the Marine Mammal Protection Act and the Endangered Species Act. Manatee management personnel of the U.S. Fish and Wildlife Service, for example, carry out consultations with other federal agencies as required by Section 7 of the Endangered Species Act to ensure that an action that is "authorized, funded, or carried out by such agency . . . is not likely to jeopardize the continued existence" of manatees or cause destruction of manatee critical habitat. As of 1987, more "jeopardy opinions" had been issued for manatees than for all other endangered species combined in the United States. The management arm of the U.S. Fish and Wildlife Service works closely with the research arm of the service (the Sirenia Project in Gainesville) to be sure that management decisions reflect the best scientific information available.

Other state and federal agencies get involved in issuing permits and regulations. To strengthen planning, regulatory, and permit programs, two important steps include:

1. Insistence by the state that local growth-management plans include measures to assure habitat quality, manatee protection and quality of human existence for the long-term; and
2. Development of consistent criteria by which all involved federal and state agencies will consider permit applications involving boating facilities (such as ramps, harbors, marinas) in essential manatee habitat.

It is particularly important for regulatory agencies to include a margin of safety to account for limitations in knowledge and imperfect human institutions.

All the laws and regulations in the world will not help manatees unless enforcement is adequate. Although both the federal and state governments have officers working to enforce rules regarding manatees, the primary enforcement agency in Florida's coastal waters is the Florida Marine Patrol (part of the Department of Natural Resources). In 1987, there were 210 field

Measures to reduce manatee injury include regulating boating speeds in areas where manatees are common. Photograph courtesy of Florida Department of Natural Resources

officers in the Marine Patrol, but an additional 250 were needed for adequate coverage of Florida's extensive coastline. Although not as dramatic, there is a need for an increased federal enforcement presence as well.

Since the mid-1970s, a number of organizations and agencies have developed materials and/or programs for education or public awareness. A few of the notable programs include those by the U.S. Fish and Wildlife Service, the Florida Department of Natural Resources, the Save the Manatee Club, Port Everglades Authority, various oceanaria or zoological parks (to be considered later in this chapter), Tampa Electric Company and various colleges and universities. Between 1977 and 1987, the organization that spent the most on manatee-oriented education and public awareness was probably Florida Power & Light Company, which spent nearly a quarter of a million dollars on educational materials during that period. The company's pamphlet entitled "Boater's Guide to Manatees" has been especially popular, with 219,000 copies distributed through mid-1987.

The multifaceted education and public awareness programs for manatees in Florida have been extremely effective, and the various agencies and organizations should be commended for their efforts to date. Some suggestions for improving education programs include developing special programs to increase boater awareness of ways to avoid watercraft-related manatee mortality and injury; providing legislators and public officials with very up-to-date information on manatee mortality, research programs and threats to manatee or their habitat; establishing a federal interpretive education center at Crystal River; and developing educational materials in Spanish, as well as English.

A relatively new tool that can enhance education, research and management efforts is a type of computer program called a Geographic Information System, or GIS. A GIS uses very precise, digitized maps, on which are plotted any of a variety of geographically referenced data sets, such as locations of dead manatees, locations where living manatees are observed, seagrass distribution and density, boat traffic patterns, locations of warm-water and freshwater discharges, boat ramps and marinas or proposed development sites. The data sets can be plotted as a series of overlays that permit easy visualization of locations where current or future human activities could have a substantial impact on manatees. Identification of such sites subsequently permits the appropriate agencies to take steps to reduce or eliminate the impact. The Marine Mammal Commission in 1989 provided funds for a workshop to evaluate whether and how GIS could be used effectively to promote management of manatees and critical manatee habitat; since that time, the Florida Department of Natural Resources and the U.S. Fish and Wildlife Service have worked closely to digitize maps and enter relevant data.

The level of interinstitutional and interagency cooperation, and the commitment to the areas of manatee research; habitat protection; regulatory,

Educational publications, like these issued by Florida Department of Natural Resources and Florida Power & Light Company, help promote public awareness of manatee conservation measures. Photographs courtesy of Florida Department of Natural Resources and Florida Power & Light Company

planning and permit activities; enforcement and education were never more apparent than during the development of a revised Florida Manatee Recovery Plan in 1988 and 1989. The Endangered Species Act requires the responsible federal agency (in the case of the manatee, that agency is the U.S. Fish and Wildlife Service) to develop a Recovery Plan for each endangered species. Accordingly, the original Florida Manatee Recovery Plan was drafted and approved on April 15, 1980. In February 1988, the Fish and Wildlife Service appointed a new Manatee Recovery Team to "update and refine the tasks presented in the original" plan.

The revised Florida Manatee Recovery Plan "is intended to serve as a guide that delineates and schedules those actions necessary to restore the Florida manatee as a viable self-sustaining element of its ecosystem." The revised plan involved considerable work by a number of people, representing a variety of organizations, and it was approved and signed by representatives of 13 government agencies and private organizations on July 24, 1989. Among other things, the plan provides an implementation schedule with prioritized tasks assigned to appropriate agencies; the tasks themselves fall into several categories, including information gathering, research, management, habitat acquisition, education and enforcement. This well-written plan, therefore, serves as an extremely important document for conserving manatees.

To summarize ideas regarding conservation of manatees in Florida, it would appear that a framework is in place: Effective legislation exists, a reasonable database has been developed, and there is good interagency and interinstitutional cooperation and commitment. The problems are that manatees die in greater and greater numbers every year, that certain human activities that kill manatees (boating, for example) increase every year and that the time may come when there are simply too few manatees in the wild to maintain a viable population. The recent state legislation is a vital step in the right direction, since it attempts to control the human activity (boating) that kills the most manatees. The real key to survival of manatees and manatee habitat, though, involves a change in human attitudes—people must perceive the need to take steps to conserve the inshore environment (including manatees) for future generations, even if it means restricting some activities of the current generations.

CONSERVATION OF MANATEES OUTSIDE FLORIDA

To be sure, conservation of manatees in Florida is no inexpensive or easy task. However, the basic components needed to conserve the subspecies are in place. The same cannot be said of manatees outside Florida. Thus, even though there may be reasonable numbers of manatees outside of Florida, their survival could be in much greater jeopardy than the Florida manatee's.

Consider some of the problems associated with conservation of Antillean, Amazonian or West African manatees. There are a number of areas in which the difficulty of launching or maintaining effective conservation programs for Florida manatees versus manatees elsewhere can be compared:

- *Coordination of conservation and management efforts.* The Florida manatee is found in one country, and the bulk of its population occupies one state. Coordination is relatively easy. The other three types of manatees are found in several contiguous countries, some of which are actually in armed conflict with each other. The coordination that provides strength for the Florida manatee programs will be very difficult to achieve for the other species, either within or among countries.

- *Commitment to conserve manatees.* The Florida Manatee Recovery Plan demonstrates commitment on the part of government agencies, private organizations and dedicated individuals to conserve manatees and their habitat. Money, as well as time, has been invested in this effort. This level of commitment is not apparent in most countries occupied by other manatees at this time. For some countries where socioeconomic conditions are poor, conserving manatees is probably not going to be a high priority for some time. One competing concern involves development of fisheries in certain countries. The fisheries can provide an important source of protein and money, but fishing nets can also incidentally take manatees, perhaps devastating local manatee populations. Resolution of this, and other, incidental-take situations must be achieved.

- *Research and availability of solid data on which to base decision.* Daniel S. Hartman began his classic study of Florida manatee behavior and ecology in the late 1960s. The Sirenia Project of the U.S. Fish and Wildlife Service began its multifaceted research program in 1974, the same year that Dan Odell began his manatee studies at the University of Miami. Thus, there exist data bases that are two-to-three decades old for Florida manatees. Such comprehensive data bases do not exist for the other manatees. In fact, the existing data for manatees outside the United States are so scanty that it is difficult to make well-informed management decisions.

- *Habitat Protection.* Although parks exist in which wildlife (including manatees) are legally protected, programs to assess and acquire critical habitat specifically for manatees (as exist in Florida) are not present elsewhere, with the exception of Guatemala. In some parts of the world (such as Amazonia) large-scale habitat destruction occurs. In other areas (for example, Gambia) damming of rivers will alter the habitat and directly and indirectly have an impact on manatees. The welfare of manatees and other wildlife must be considered as projects that alter or destroy habitat are considered.

- *Planning and regulatory activities.* Aside from the activities for Florida manatees, such efforts appear to be confined to creating parks that will reduce the impact of humans. Creation of parks is a commendable activity, but the extent to which parks include habitat critical to manatees specifically, is not known.

- *Enforcement of laws designed to protect manatees.* Enforcement programs are certainly understaffed in the United States, but the situation is much worse in areas occupied by the other manatees, despite protective legislation in all countries where manatees exist. Thus, even though manatees are theoretically protected, in some countries manatee meat is openly sold in markets. The most comprehensive legal protection cannot succeed if there is inadequate inforcement.

- *Education.* The other component needed to conserve a species is education of the general public as to why and how to save that species. Education programs have been excellent for Florida manatees, although even greater effectiveness could be achieved. Manatee education and public awareness programs have been less strong for manatees outside Florida, where the education aspect of conservation may be particularly important because manatees are considered an excellent source of meat and other products.

Thus, it appears that countries interested in conserving manatees must work hard and work quickly to do so. These countries must make a commitment for the long term, but they must begin acquiring biological data, setting aside critical habitat and enforcing protective legislation before local manatee populations dwindle further.

CONSERVATION OF DUGONGS

The dugong, like the West African and Antillean manatees, exists in the territorial waters of many nations. While the dugong is protected by many national laws, the sheer number of laws and differing degrees of effectiveness preclude easily coordinated enforcement and result in ineffective protection for the dugong and some seriously reduced populations. In many countries, economic factors may contribute to ineffective enforcement, even though the government is genuinely interested in protecting dugongs. Fortunately, a large proportion of the remaining population occurs within the jurisdiction of a single country (Australia). Other relatively large populations (such as those in the Persian Gulf) will require multinational cooperation to ensure adequate protection. This is particularly difficult when, as in this case, their habitat is the site of international hostilities.

Protection of the dugong must go beyond simply the passage and enforcement of laws. People must be convinced that the dugong is an important part of nature that must be preserved for future generations. In some nations such as Australia and Papua New Guinea, the dugong is important in native tradition and culture. Here, dugong conservation is approached using modern research and management techniques (e.g., aerial surveys, telemetry, habitat protection) coupled with an education program, to allow traditional hunting to continue. Even traditional hunting should be subject to catch quotas, and hunters should be encouraged to be selective in

Dugong conservation efforts must combine education programs and accommodation of traditional hunting practices. Photograph by Alice J. Monroe

*Manatees eating water hyacinth. The animals use their
pectoral (front) flippers to push vegetation into their mouths.*
Photographs by Patrick M. Rose

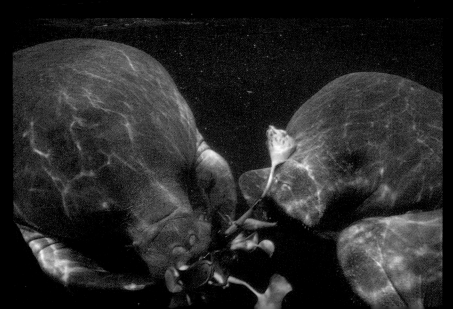

The U.S. Fish and Wildlife Service has pioneered the use of radio and satellite telemetry with sirenians such as this manatee in Florida. The transmitter rests at the surface, with its antenna exposed. The transmitter is attached around the tail stock. The belt will break if the apparatus becomes entangled and the manatee struggles. In addition, the belt corrodes and eventually breaks, so that the attachment is not permanent. Photograph courtesy of the U.S. Fish and Wildlife Service, Sirenia Project

Florida manatees' low tolerance to cold weather causes them to gather in large numbers at natural and artificial warm-water discharges. Here, a group of about 230 manatees bask in the discharge of the Riviera plant, along Florida's east coast. Photograph courtesy of John E. Reynolds III and Florida Power & Light Company

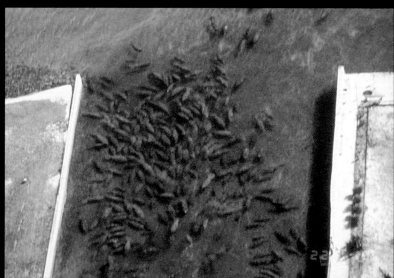

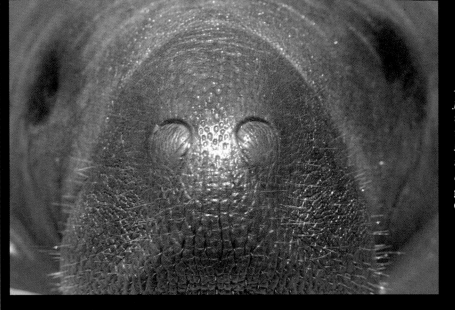

A close-up view of the face of a Florida manatee shows the vibrissae (hairs) that serve a sensory function, and the texture of the skin. Photograph by Daniel K. Odell

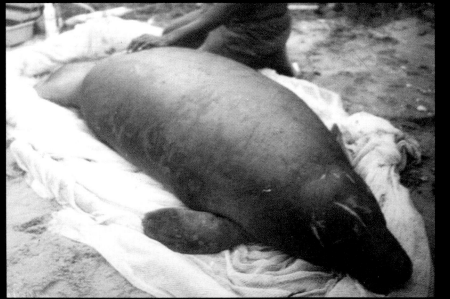

A West African manatee has been captured so that scientists can examine it. Photograph by James A. Powell

The head of this young West African manatee is similar to that of other manatees, especially the West Indian species. However, the West African manatee has more protuberant eyes and a blunter snout than its West Indian relative. Photograph by Thomas J. O'Shea

A manatee trap is located near the mouth of the River Go, in the Ivory Coast. Photograph by Thomas J. O'Shea

Amazonian manatees are smaller and darker than the West Indian species.

The white belly patches on this young Amazonian manatee are individually distinctive. Most Amazonian manatees, and even occasional Florida manatees, have such patches. Photograph by Daryl P. Domning

A manatee hunter in Careiro, Brazil, stands in his canoe. Photograph by Daryl P. Domning

Dugong swimming in Shark Bay, Australia. Photograph by Anthony Preen

Dugongs swimming in Shark Bay, Australia. Photograph by Paul K. Anderson

A resting dugong in Shark Bay displays crisscrossing scars on its back, apparently inflicted by other dugongs during mating. Photograph by Anthony Preen

Dugong at Toba Aquarium, Japan. Photograph by Daryl P. Domning

Dugong at Toba Aquarium, Japan. Note the protruding tusks. Photographs by Daryl P. Domning

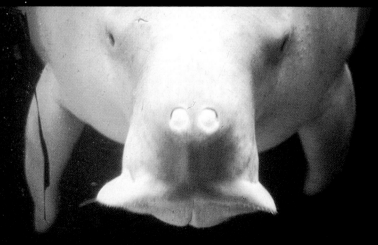

A massive group of over 600 dugongs was spotted in the Arabian Gulf. What brought these animals together in such large numbers is unknown. Photograph by Anthony Preen

A speared dugong is pulled into a boat by Bardi hunters. Photograph courtesy of Great Barrier Reef Marine Park Authority

An educational poster about sirenians. Public awareness programs play an important part in manatee conservation. Photograph courtesy of Florida Department of Natural Resources

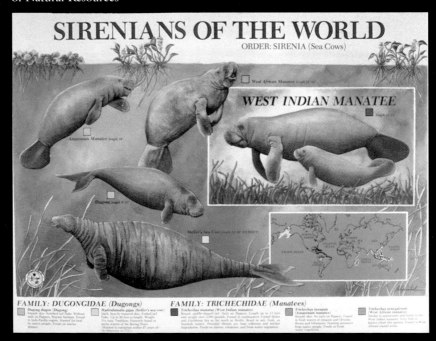

Manatee #CRO2 (top) is a male that has been sighted at Crystal River, Florida since 1977. Manatees can be identified by distinctive scar patterns inflicted by boat propellers. Photograph courtesy of the U.S. Fish and Wildlife Service, Sirenia Project

Manatee (bottom) with disfiguring scars. Photograph by Patrick M. Rose

The birth of a manatee at the Miami Seaquarium. Such births in captivity are rare.
Photograph courtesy of Miami Seaquarium

A baby manatee nuzzles its mother at the Miami Seaquarium. The "fetal folds" near the baby's tail indicate that it is close to newborn. Photograph by John E. Reynolds III

their catch to avoid pregnant females or females with dependent calves. Inclusion of aboriginal communities in the formulation of the management plan is important to the success of the plan; this has been done under the aegis of the Great Barrier Reef Marine Park Authority.

Other components of any management plan must include elimination or control of other human activities, including coastal development or oil spills that have an impact on the dugong or its habitat. For example, there is some indication that boating activity may affect dugong behavior. While the situation is not yet as serious as the watercraft problem is for manatees in Florida, experience dictates that appropriate actions should be taken to ensure that it does not become a similar danger in Australia.

Helene Marsh and her colleagues have pointed out the need to protect dugong habitat from various human activities. The Great Barrier Reef Marine Park Authority is important in an area where large numbers of dugongs, as well as dense seagrass beds that support those dugongs, receive protection. In certain countries such as India and Sri Lanka, dugong reserves have actually been recommended for particular locations, but civil unrest, poverty and problems associated with human population growth have apparently caused the governments to downplay dugong conservation. In Australia, where so many dugongs live, a series of seasonal or year-round dugong reserves could be established to ensure for posterity that the critical habitats and large populations of these wonderful animals would suffer minimally from the consequences of human activities.

THE ROLE OF OCEANARIA AND ZOOLOGICAL PARKS IN CONSERVING SIRENIANS

Over the years, zoological parks have come to play an increasingly important role in the conservation of many species of threatened and endangered animals. In some cases such as the Przewalski horse or the California condor, the entire world population of a species is maintained in zoological parks. The last California condors were specifically captured to form the nucleus of a breeding colony, because attempts to promote increased reproduction in the wild were not successful. Many other species are held in captive populations that may represent a significant proportion of the world populations because habitat destruction has left them no place to live. Captive husbandry (including breeding) programs are extremely important in maintaining the genetic diversity of small populations of endangered species. In some cases, as with the golden lion tamarin, captive breeding has been so successful that animals have been reintroduced back into their natural habitat in areas where the threat of habitat destruction is minimal or absent.

FACILITIES HOLDING SIRENIANS

Dugong
- Kebun Binatang Surabaya, Surabaya, Indonesia*
- Toba Aquarium, Toba City, Japan
- Gelanggang Samudra, Jaya Ancol Jalan, Lodan Timur, Jakarta, Indonesia

Amazonian Manatee
- Atagawa Tropical & Alligator Garden, Higashi-Izu, Japan*
- Yomiuriland Marine Aquarium, Tokyo, Japan*
- INPA, Projeto Peixe-Boi, Manaus, Brazil
- Museu Pargense Emílio Goeldi, Belém, Brazil

Antillean Manatee
- Stichting Koninklijk Zoologisch Genootschap Natura Artis Magistra, Amsterdam, Netherlands*   B
- Guyana Zoological Park, Georgetown, Guyana*
- Tiergarten der Stadt Nürnberg, Nürnberg, Germany*   B
- Aquario de Valencia, Valencia, Venezuela*
- Beijing Zoological Gardens, Beijing, People's Republic of China   B
- Okinawa Expo Memorial Park Aquarium, Motobu, Japan   B
- Zoológico Regional Miguel Alvarez del Toro, Tuxtla Gutiérrez, México
- Parqueológico José N. Revirosa, Emiliano Zapata, Tabasco, México

Florida Manatee
- Miami Seaquarium, Miami, Florida, United States   B~
- Bradenton Museum, Bradenton, Florida, United States
- The Living Seas, EPCOT, Walt Disney World, Lake Buena Vista, Florida, United States   B
- Homosassa Springs State Wildlife Park, Homosassa Springs, Florida, United States   B
- Sea World of Florida, Orlando, Florida, United States   B~
- Lowry Park Zoo, Tampa, Florida, United States   ~

---

*   Data from *International Zoo Yearbook*, vol. 28, 1989.
B   Breeding has occurred at the facility.
~   Population size varies due to rehabilitation program.

In addition to providing refuges for endangered species, zoological parks provide an opportunity to study many aspects of a species' biology that are impossible or very difficult (due to logistics or great expense) to study in the natural habitat. Learning about an animal's life history is absolutely necessary for understanding the species' biology and, when necessary, implementing sound conservation practices.

Marine zoological parks play an important role in the overall conservation strategy of sirenians by providing an opportunity to document those aspects of sirenian life history that are difficult to study in the wild. Because sirenians are considered threatened or endangered under various international and national laws, few are currently held in captivity except in research or rehabilitation programs. The largest number of captive sirenians is held in Florida in rehabilitation programs, where sick or injured manatees, captured in the wild, are brought to recover. The ultimate goal of the programs is to return manatees to their natural habitat as soon as they have recovered from their illnesses or injuries. During the rehabilitation program (which may last only a few weeks or as much as several years), scientists have the opportunity to learn much about basic manatee biology and to use the program to educate the public about the plight of the manatee in Florida (through press releases and tours of the rehabilitation facility).

Three facilities in Florida (the Miami Seaquarium, Sea World of Florida in Orlando and Lowry Park Zoo in Tampa) are specifically authorized by the U.S. Fish and Wildlife Service to rehabilitate manatees. The facilities donate almost all of the funds (for staff time, water, electricity, veterinary care, food) necessary to run the program. For example, since 1976, Sea World has made over 90 responses to reports of sick, injured or orphaned manatees. Twenty-seven animals have been released; 13 are still undergoing rehabilitation; and the remainder died due to the severity of their injuries or advanced state of disease. Manatees that are released are given individual identification marks (freeze-brands) and often fitted with VHF or satellite radio transmitters under the supervision of U.S. Fish and Wildlife Service personnel. Federal and state biologists track released animals to be sure that they reintegrate into manatee "society." To date all of the releases have been successful. Orphans are not currently being released because they have not had an opportunity to learn seasonal migratory pathways and the sites of warm-water refuges. Orphans may eventually be released, under well-regulated conditions, to determine whether they can easily readapt to the wild. This is not likely to occur in Florida, however, until the problem of watercraft collisions has been resolved.

The joint efforts of these marine zoological parks, in cooperation with federal and state agencies, continue to gather essential information on manatee biology that is helping to define the role of the manatee in the coastal ecosystem and provide some of the basic data on the manatee's life history that are necessary for proper conservation plans. During the rehabilitation program, there is an opportunity to document how sick or injured manatees respond to antibiotics; the best way to handle them for blood collection, X-rays, and tube feeding; what kind of milk formula is best for orphans; how often they have to be fed; how fast they grow; and what "normal" blood chemistry is. Captive animals are also available for other, noninvasive studies, including DNA fingerprinting and manatee acoustics. Manatees have reproduced in several oceanaria around the world. Observations of behavior of captive female/calf pairs provides insight into such behavior in wild manatees.

The first manatee conceived and born in captivity in the United States was born in 1975 at the Miami Seaquarium. The baby, named Lorelei, created considerable excitement. Interested scientists and laypersons witnessed the baby's early efforts to swim with its mother, Juliet, and the bonding that occurred as the two nuzzled and vocalized to one another. Shortly after birth, Lorelei's coordination and buoyancy were not perfected, and it was comical to watch as she energetically sculled with her pectoral flippers to stay near her mother. Later, Lorelei's growth and development were monitored, as well as her relationship with other manatees at the Seaquarium. Today, Lorelei is an adult, who has herself produced calves.

The sirenians held in captivity also provide insight for scientists whose goals include preservation of the various sirenian species. The insight into manatee biology has led directly to successful treatment and rehabilitation of injured or diseased animals. Further, the captive sirenians can be useful to educate the public about their biology and conservation. Clearly, marine zoological parks have provided a unique forum for the specialist and the layperson to learn about and appreciate manatees and dugongs.

In the October 1987 issue of *Sirenews* Daryl Domning addressed the subject of breeding manatees in captivity to restock animals killed as a result of human activities. As Dr. Domning rightfully pointed out, the problem is not that manatees are not breeding in the wild; the problem is that mortality is excessive. Raising manatees in a captive setting produces animals that are inexperienced with, and therefore vulnerable to, watercraft and other human activities, and seasonal cold weather and the resultant need to migrate to warm-water discharges. Placing such animals in the wild would probably condemn them to death from human activities or the cold. Thus, breeding of manatees in captivity to restock the wild population is inappropriate. The key to survival of manatees in the wild is to reduce direct mortality due to human activities, as well as to maintain critical habitat.

However, breeding manatees in captivity under controlled conditions to study manatee reproductive biology is an appropriate course of action. Manatees breed rather well in captivity, yet little has been learned about their reproductive biology; for example the gestation period has not been properly documented. The key working phrase is "under controlled conditions." This means there should be a well-conceived plan that documents reproductive behavior and physiology as well as the birth, growth and development of the calves. The captive environment is well suited to this task and these studies would make a significant addition to our knowledge of manatee and dugong biology.

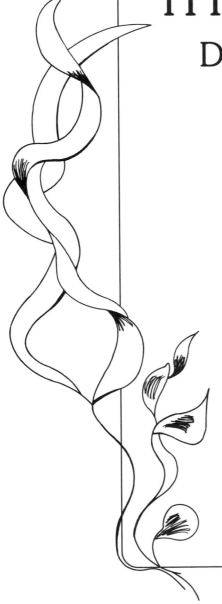

WHY SAVE
THE MANATEE?

Daryl P. Domning

Most residents of Florida must be aware by now of the strenuous efforts being made to save the Florida manatee from extinction; and some may indeed wonder why this is being done. Different people from different backgrounds will answer this question in different ways. Here, I give my own answers, the ones I have arrived at after some 20 years of scientific study of manatees and their relatives. In my opinion, these reasons more than justify every effort we are making to protect not only manatees, but living species and their habitats in general. For we cannot consider the manatee just by itself; though the manatee is unique, its problems are not. In the long run, to save any endangered species, we must deal with the basic problems that have put all of them, and us, in the same leaking boat. And surely it is in our own interest to make sure their end of the boat does not sink.

Among the reasons for protecting manatees in particular, I would list the following, roughly in order of increasing importance:

1. Manatees are fascinating animals, and people enjoy seeing them and learning about them. Many people come to Florida just to see manatees in public aquaria, at Crystal River, Homosassa Springs, Blue Spring State Park, power-plant outfalls or elsewhere in the wild. Rarely, especially in the eastern United States, can people come into such close proximity with large wild animals, without risk of injury and in such an enjoyable and rewarding fashion. The new knowledge about the manatee's life cycle and habits that we scientists gain from research is disseminated in films, newspapers and magazines that entertain and inform millions of people, enriching our culture just as do contributions to the arts and humanities. Everyone can agree that an Africa without elephants would make the earth a less interesting place to live; the same goes for a Florida without manatees.

2. Manatees eat introduced aquatic weeds, such as hydrilla and water hyacinth, which infest Florida's waterways. Efforts to use them systematically for weed clearance may not prove feasible, but without manatees, state and local governments would have to spend more on aquatic weed control, in many cases using toxic herbicides. Manatees help do the job for free and without polluting their (and our) environment.

3. For millions of years, manatees have been a natural part of our estuaries and nearshore marine environments. These in turn harbor living communities, such as seagrass beds, which contribute to our own food, water and oxygen supply and our general well-being. For example, these marine communities are vital breeding and feeding grounds of commercially important shellfish and finfish. They also absorb environmental contaminants, thereby helping to clean our waters. And like the coal

miners' canary, they act as early warning systems and first lines of defense against our ecological mistakes: Sometimes the harmful effects of pollution or other damage we do to our environment show up in these areas before they have a direct impact on humans. Therefore, we all have a stake in the continued health of these natural communities and the living organisms they comprise.

Although scientists recognize the interdependence of species within ecosystems, we do not yet understand all the ways that manatees contribute to these communities. It is likely, however, that their feeding and defecation speed up the recycling of nutrients and stimulate the growth of many aquatic plants and animals, including those of commercial value. We would be very foolish if we extirpated manatees in Florida before we fully understood how we benefit from their presence.

4. The age of genetic engineering is just dawning; in the coming century, genetic resources will be as much in commercial demand as oil and gas resources are today. Ironically, it is just at this time that we are wiping out living species at a rate never before equaled, destroying genetic diversity that took millions of years to create and that cannot ever be recreated. Already, many of our important drugs and industrial materials are of plant or animal origin, and most of the millions of living species have never even been investigated for possible uses of this kind. We may be certain that many of them harbor substances that will prove useful in curing diseases, such as cancer or AIDS, or that will spawn some new industry as yet undreamed of. In addition, the very loss of a species may create a new problem if, unknown to us, it was keeping in check some other creature that now explodes out of control. Each time we destroy a species, we play Russian roulette with our own future. As the only herbivorous marine mammal in North and Central America, the manatee and its unique genetic makeup already benefit us in the ways mentioned above. For all we know, manatees may have the potential to provide still other genetic resources of future value to us. Their circulatory systems, physiology and digestive chemistry differ from those of most other animals, and their bones are unusually dense, suggesting that their thyroid metabolism may also prove to be unusual. It would not be surprising if they turned out to produce substances useful to our pharmaceutical industry, or if their physiology shed light on the processes of cardiovascular disease, bone diseases or other ailments in humans. But the painstaking research necessary to explore these possibilities will take decades, or even generations, to accomplish. On our present course, we and the Florida manatee may not have that much time left.

5. Through evolution, we are blood relatives of every other species. They are our extended family in the most inclusive sense; hence, they are parts of us, both physically and psychologically, just as our own families are. We are only beginning to appreciate how profoundly our physical and psychological development is influenced by our experiences in early childhood. How much less, therefore, do we understand the subtle influences that our evolutionary history might have had on those aspects of our mental and other functions that are inherited.

Consider the health of our bodies: Compared with the millions of years during which our ancestors lived in what we now call "wilderness," the time we have spent in houses and cities is negligible. This means that the environment to which we are biologically adapted is not an environment made up of plastic and automobiles, but one made up of plants and animals. No wonder that more and more of the synthetic substances we consume and expose ourselves to are turning out to cause cancer: Our bodies were never designed to run on such stuff. Even radon, a natural substance that was never a problem before, is now causing us trouble simply because we live in poorly ventilated houses.

We may be taking similar risks with our minds when we are denied the kinds of stimulation and the release from stress that access to the "natural" world provides. Monkeys forced to live their lives in small, sterile cages show obvious signs of insanity. How much of the human behavior reported in our newspapers has a similar cause? How much of the violence, drug addiction and general nastiness that beset so much urban life are the mental diseases of a species locked up away from its natural surroundings? We simply don't know.

What we do know is that we are to a great extent, products of our environment, both as individuals and as a species. We evolved from and within a biological context, and therefore this context is necessarily imprinted in our genes and in our character. We (some of us, at least) feel this instinctively—a feeling that Harvard biologist E.O. Wilson calls "biophilia": our natural affinity for living things. It shows itself in many ways: the pets and house plants we surround ourselves with, the lawns and gardens we tend, the parks and zoos we build, the hunting and fishing trips we take, the expensive vacations to forest retreats and other wild places (for example, to Florida to dive with manatees). All help us relax and escape from stress.

The deeper implications of this for our psychology have not yet been explored. But there's more to it than just aesthetics, need for recreation or a superficial fondness for cute animals. It's already clear that the artificial urban environments that so many people live in, remote from most wildlife other than rats and pigeons, threaten to warp and deaden the human spirit that created them. An urbanized planet, a planet with no space for wild manatees, will also not have space enough for what human beings are meant to be. This is part of the reason why people so avidly seek out, not just living things, not just zoos and pets, but wilderness and wildlife. We cannot fully develop our humanness if we spend our whole lives cut off from our own natural context, caged in our cities like the animals in our zoos. In short, the survival of other species *and their habitats* is necessary to our mental health.

6. All the above reasons for saving manatees, or other species, have one thing in common: They are all based on what those creatures can or might do for us. But as a scientist and as a human being, I am convinced that this is not the whole story. There is a further reason, not economic, pragmatic, or human-centered, but the most compelling of all.

There are some things for which civilized people simply do not demand economic justification. Aid is sent to starving Africans, not with a view to anticipated return, but because they are starving. Humane treatment of animals is mandated by law because our society has deemed it right, even if it costs more. Over the centuries we have developed a consensus that some things just ought to be done, and this list of moral desiderata has slowly grown. Murder and theft should be outlawed, slavery and torture should be abolished, racial discrimination and genocide should be banned. Though these practices continue, at least most societies now acknowledge them to be crimes. Extermination of a species is also a crime. It is murder of a unique and irreplaceable evolutionary "individual"; it is theft at the expense of our own descendants; and it is a form of genocide as indefensible as any other.

In other words, we humans, as the *de facto* stewards of nature, are morally accountable for our stewardship. At the very least, we are accountable to posterity, and for the blunders we have already committed with toxic and radioactive wastes, we may even live to be cursed by our own children. Those who acknowledge an authority above and beyond this world have still more reason to fear judgment. But if we pride ourselves on any claim to morality at all, whatever its philosophical basis, that morality must lead us to use nature in a way that will preserve its diversity permanently intact. The extermination of species, and the communities they are part of, is not only against our own interests, but an intolerable crime against life itself.

7. We can also approach the problem of saving manatees from the opposite, negative side: Is there any excuse for not doing it? Clayton E. Ray of the Smithsonian Institution has pointed out that, notwithstanding the currently enormous popularity of marine mammals in general, there is even

less excuse for failure to preserve Florida manatees than almost any other marine mammal. Unlike polar bears, they are not dangerous to man. Unlike bowhead whales, dugongs or even other manatee populations, they are not game for subsistence hunters. Unlike porpoises, seals and sea otters, they do not compete with our commercial and recreational fisheries. Unlike whales, they are not at the center of international disputes. Compared with most other marine mammals, they are accessible to biologists for study and are relatively well-known scientifically. They are even relatively tolerant of humans, and live on the doorstep of one of the most affluent, sophisticated and conservation-minded human populations. Like Al Capp's shmoo, a more harmless and accommodating animal could not be imagined. What excuse could we give for its extinction? If as citizens of the United States, we cannot save manatees in Florida, we cannot expect anyone to save any species anywhere. And (needless to say) the U.S. citizens ultimately responsible for the Florida manatee are the people of Florida.

But if it is so easy to give reasons for saving manatees, why is it so hard to actually do it? What threats do they, in fact, face? Why does anyone threaten the existence of such harmless creatures? For several reasons, but ultimately for just one reason. Manatees and their relatives are hunted for food in many Third World countries with growing and increasingly hungry populations. They are killed as agricultural pests in West Africa, where growing human populations extend their rice fields into the manatees' habitat and the manatees welcome the rice as a supplement to their diet. They are killed in gillnets and other fishing gear used increasingly around the world to feed other growing human populations. They are killed in Florida by floodgates and locks built to provide dry building sites, agricultural land and commercial navigation for the fastest-growing state in our nation. They are killed most of all by the growing numbers of commercial and recreational boats in Florida: nearly a million of them today, 2 million by the year 2000, not counting out-of-state visitors. It is not the manatees' hides we covet, therefore, but their habitat. Manatees (like wildlife in general) are being crowded off the earth by human beings.

The steady flow of new residents into Florida (now some 1,000 each day) is unavoidably degrading the state's environment for people and wildlife alike. This bears repeating: Unlimited population growth and "development" of the sort now taking place in Florida *cannot* be reconciled with protection of wildlife and the environment. The Florida panther will probably be the first species to go; then others, including the manatee. If this is to be averted, hard political and economic decisions—unpopular decisions—will have to be made. Stronger legislation will be needed, not just to plan for future growth but to *stop* quantitative growth measured in sheer numbers of people, buildings, roads, boats and marinas. We must learn to reject this harmful, cancerlike growth in favor of *qualitative* growth: ongoing improvement in the lives of our people, in the context of a healthy environment. There are so many kinds of growth and development we need that do not require new building sites or more dredge-and-fill projects: instead of more housing, better housing, better schools, better services of every sort.

The United States, and particularly Florida, are already overpopulated; yet most people still refuse to believe this. We need leaders with the vision and courage to show them the danger and give them an alternative to our present self-destructive course. Like it or not, we will be judged by historians of the future, and judged to a great extent on our answer to one question: Are we willing to share our space with manatees and other species, even if it requires us to make sacrifices and limit the number of people who can live and play here?

The politically easy answer to this question is the wrong answer.

The preceding chapter was written by Daryl P. Domning for the U.S. Marine Mammal Commission in Washington, D.C. (The Commission kindly permitted use of the paper to enhance this book.) Readers should note that, although Domning focuses on reasons to conserve manatees in Florida, his arguments apply equally to the other species of sirenians.

SELECTED NON-GOVERNMENTAL ORGANIZATIONS INVOLVED IN CONSERVATION OF SIRENIANS

The Belize Zoo
P.O. Box 474
Belize City, Belize
Central America

Florida Power & Light Company
Environmental Affairs
P.O. Box 14000
Juno Beach, Florida 33408

Save the Manatee Club
500 North Maitland Avenue
Suite #210
Maitland, Florida 32751

Tampa Electric Company
P.O. Box 111
Tampa, Florida 33601-0111

United Nations Environment
  Programme
P.O. Box 30552
Nairobi, Kenya

Wildlife Conservation International
Building A
New York Zoological Society
Bronx, New York 10460

The World Conservation Union
Ave. du Mont-Blanc
CH-1196 Gland
Switzerland

World Wildlife Fund
1250 24th Street N.W.
Washington, D.C. 20037

LEGAL STATUS OF SIRENIANS

Red Data Books

The World Conservation Union (formerly the International Union for the Conservation of Nature and Natural Resources) attempts to document endangered species and to work to maintain sustainable populations of them. The union publishes the Red Data Books, in which species are classified as endangered (likely to become extinct if nothing changes), vulnerable (likely to become endangered if nothing changes; includes species whose populations are decreasing and/or whose habitat is being steadily lost throughout the range), rare (in no danger, but not common), out of danger and indeterminate. In 1972, the Amazonian manatee was listed as endangered, with the rest of the sirenians being listed as vulnerable; in 1982, all four species of sirenian were listed as vulnerable.

Convention on International Trade in Endangered Species of Wild Fauna and Flora (CITES)

Since 1975, CITES has provided an international framework for regulating trade in plants and animals that either are or may be threatened with extinction. The United States and 102 other countries are parties to CITES. The convention lists species in three appendices. Species listed under Appendix I are threatened with extinction. Those under Appendix II are not necessarily threatened with extinction at present, but may be if trade is not strictly controlled. Species listed under Appendix III include any plants or animals that a party subjects to regulation within its jurisdiction for the purpose of restricting or preventing exploitation.

The dugong is listed under Appendix I, except in Australia, where it is listed under Appendix II. The Amazonian and West Indian manatee (both subspecies) appear under Appendix I. The West African manatee is listed under Appendix II.

Other International Protection

The West African manatee is protected under Class A of the African Convention for the Conservation of Nature and Natural Resources. Thirty eight African countries originally signed this convention, which took effect in 1969, and which requires total protection for all Class A species.

The United States Endangered Species Act provides protection for species that are either currently endangered or threatened with extinction. The act prohibits taking (defined as harassing, harming, pursuing, hunting, shooting, wounding, killing, trapping, capturing, collecting or attempting any of the foregoing), trading, processing and transport, both *within and outside* the United States. Dugongs were listed December 2, 1970, as endangered; West Indian and Amazonian manatees were listed on June 2, 1970, as endangered; and the West African manatee was listed on July 20, 1979, as threatened.

Protection in Specific Countries

It appears that the sirenians are protected to some extent by national or local acts in every country they occupy. In some countries, more than one act protects sirenians; in the United States, for example, the Federal Marine Mammal Protecton Act of 1972 and Endangered Species Act of 1973 both provide protection for sirenians, and the state of Florida passed the Manatee Sanctuary Act of 1978 to provide additional protection. Many countries have legislation that predates those just listed by many years; for example, manatees in Guyana have been legally protected by Fisheries Ordinance No. 30 since 1956, and Ivory Coast enacted Loi No. 65-255 (Protection de la Fauna) in 1965.

SELECTED READINGS

The following list of references serves two primary purposes. Most importantly, the list includes sources used in writing particular chapters of the book, and especially some sources quoted in the text. The references also are listed to provide interested readers with additional sources of information. Readers should note that we list each reference only once, generally under the first chapter it was used where we feel it was particularly relevant.

Introduction
Norris, K.S. 1978. Marine mammals and man. pp. 320–338. *Wildlife and America*, ed. H.P. Brokaw. Council on Environmental Quality.

The Evolution of Manatees and Dugongs
de Jong, W., A. Zweers and M. Goodman. 1981. Relationship of aardvarks to elephants, hyraxes, and sea cows from alpha-crystallin sequences. *Nature* 292(5823):538–540.

Domning, D.P. 1977. An ecological model for late Tertiary sirenian evolution in the North Pacific Ocean. *Systematic Zoology* 25(4):352–362.

———. 1981. Sea cows and sea grasses. *Paleobiology* 7(4):417–420.

———. 1982. Evolution of manatees: a speculative history. *Journal of Paleontology* 56(3):599–619.

———. 1989. Kelp evolution: a comment. *Paleobiology* 15(1):53–56.

Domning, D.P., and L.C. Hayek. 1986. Interspecific and intraspecific morphological variation in manatees (Sirenia: *Trichechus*). *Marine Mammal Science* 2(2):87–144.

Reinhart, R.H. 1976. Fossil sirenians and desmostylids from Florida and elsewhere. *Bulletin of the Florida State Museum, Biological Sciences* 20(4):187–300.

People, Manatees and Dugongs

Allsopp, W.H.L. 1961. Putting manatees to work. *New Scientist* no. 263:548–549.

———. 1969. Aquatic weed control by manatees—its prospects and problems. pp. 344–351. *Man-Made Lakes: The Accra Symposium.* ed. L.E. Obeng. Ghana Universities Press, Accra.

Baughman, J.L. 1946. Some early notices on American manatees and the mode of their capture. *Journal of Mammalogy* 27(3):234–239.

Chase, A. 1981. Dugongs and Australian indigenous cultural systems: some introductory remarks. pp. 112–122. *The Dugong.* ed. H. Marsh. Proceedings of a seminar/workshop, May 8–13, 1979 at James Cook University of North Queensland, Townsville, Australia.

Cropp, B. 1982. Timeless hunters. *Oceans* 15(6):16–20.

Domning, D.P. 1982. Commercial exploitation of manatees *Trichechus* in Brazil c. 1785–1973. *Biological Conservation* 22:101–126.

Etheridge, K., et al. 1985. Consumption of aquatic plants by the West Indian manatee. *Journal of Aquatic Plant Management* 23:21–25.

Hudson, B.E.T. 1980. Dugongs in Papua New Guinea: West New Britain. *Wildlife in Papua New Guinea.*

Lefebvre, L.W., T.J. O'Shea, G.B. Rathbun and R.C. Best. 1989. Distribution, status, and biogeography of the West Indian manatee. pp. 567–610. *Biogeography of the West Indies,* ed. C.A. Woods. Gainesville, Fla. Sandhill Crane Press.

MacLaren, J.P. 1967. Manatees as a naturalistic biological mosquito control method. *Mosquito News* 27(3):387–393.

National Science Research Council. 1974. An international centre for manatee research. Report of a workshop, February 7–13, 1974, Georgetown, Guyana.

Nietschmann, B., and J. Nietschmann. 1981. Good dugong, bad dugong; bad turtle, good turtle. *Natural History* 90(5):54–63.

O'Shea, T.J. 1988. The past, present, and future of manatees in the southeastern United States: realities, misunderstandings, and enigmas. pp. 184–204. *Proceedings of the Third Southeastern Nongame and Endangered Wildlife*

Symposium. ed. R.R. Odom et al. Georgia Dept. Natural Resources, Game and Fish Division, Social Circle.

Peterson, S.L. 1974. Man's relationship with the Florida manatee, *Trichechus manatus latirostris* (Harlan): an historical perspective. M.A. thesis, University of Michigan.

Reynolds, J.E. III, and J.R. Wilcox. 1987. People, power plants, and manatees. *Sea Frontiers* 33(4):263–269.

Sguros, P. 1966. Use of the Florida manatee as an agent for the suppression of aquatic and bankweed growth in essential inland waterways. Research rept. and extension proposal submitted to Central and Southern Florida Flood Control Board.

The Florida Manatee

Brownell Jr., R.L., and K. Ralls (eds.). 1981. The West Indian manatee in Florida. Proceedings of a workshop, March 27–29, 1978, Orlando, Fla. Florida Dept. Natural Resources, Tallahassee.

Caldwell, D.K., and M.C. Caldwell. 1985. Manatees—*Trichechus manatus, Trichechus senegalensis,* and *Trichechus inunguis.* pp. 33–36. *Handbook of Marine Mammals,* vol. 3, *The Sirenians and Baleen Whales.* eds. S.H. Ridgway and R.J. Harrison. London: Academic Press.

Hartman, D.S. 1969. Florida's manatees, mermaids in peril. *National Geographic* 136(3):342–353.

———. 1979. Ecology and behavior of the manatee (*Trichechus manatus*) in Florida. Special publication no. 5, American Society of Mammalogists.

Husar, S.L. 1977. The West Indian manatee *Trichechus manatus.* Wildlife research report 7, U.S. Dept. of the Interior, Fish and Wildlife Service, Washington, D.C.

———. 1978. *Trichechus manatus. Mammalian Species,* no. 93:5pp.

Irvine, A.B. 1983. Manatee metabolism and its influence on distribution in Florida. *Biological Conservation* 25:315–334.

McClenaghan, L.R., and T.J. O'Shea. 1988. Genetic variability in the Florida manatee (*Trichechus manatus*). *Journal of Mammalogy* 69(3):481–488.

Odell, D.K. 1982. West Indian manatee *Trichechus manatus.* pp. 828–837. *Wild Mammals of North America: Biology, Management and Economics,* eds. J.A. Chapman and G.A. Feldhamer. Baltimore: The Johns Hopkins University Press.

Odell, D.K., and J.E. Reynolds III. 1979. Observations on manatee mortality in South Florida. *Journal of Wildlife Management* 43(2):572–577.

Odell, D.K., J.E. Reynolds III and G. Waugh. 1978. New records of the West Indian manatee (*Trichechus manatus*) from the Bahama Islands. *Biological Conservation* 14:289–293.

O'Shea, T.J., J.F. Moore and H.I. Kochman. 1984. Contaminant concentrations in manatees in Florida. *Journal of Wildlife Management* 48(3):741–748.

O'Shea, T.J., et al. 1985. An analysis of manatee mortality patterns in Florida, 1976–1981. *Journal of Wildlife Management* 49(1):1–11.

Reynolds, J.E. III. 1979. The semisocial manatee. *Natural History* 88(2):44–53

Reynolds, J.E. III, and J.R. Wilcox. 1986. Distribution and abundance of the West Indian manatee *Trichechus manatus* around selected Florida power plants following winter cold fronts: 1984–1985. *Biological Conservation* 38:103–113.

Van Meter, V.B. 1987. The West Indian manatee in Florida. Florida Power & Light Company, Juno Beach, Florida.

The Antillean Manatee

Belitsky, D.W., and C.L. Belitsky. 1980. Distribution and abundance of manatees (*Trichechus manatus*) in the Dominican Republic. *Biological Conservation* 17:313–319.

Colmenero-Rolon, L.C. 1985. Aspectos de la ecología y comportamiento de una colonia de manaties (*Trichechus manatus*) en el Municipio de Emiliano Zapata, Tabasco. *An. Inst. Biol. Univ. Nat. Auton. Méx.*, 56, Zool. Ser. (2):589–602.

Colmenero-Rolon, L.C., and B.E. Zarate. 1990. Distribution, status and conservation of the West Indian manatee in Quintana Roo, Mexico. *Biological Conservation* 52:27–35.

Colmenero-Rolon, L.C., and M.E.H. Zavala. 1986. Distribución de los manaties, situación y su conservación en México. *An. Inst. Biol. Univ. Nat. Auton. Méx.*, 56, Zool. Ser. (3):955–1020.

Fairbairn, P.W., and A.M. Haynes. 1982. Jamaican surveys of the West Indian manatee (*Trichechus manatus*), dolphin (*Tursiops truncatus*), and sea turtles (families Cheloniidae and Dermochelyidae) and booby terns (family Laridae). UN FAO *Fisheries Report* 278:289–295.

Freeman, J., and H. Quintero. 1990. The distribution of West Indian manatees (*Trichechus manatus*) in Puerto Rico. National Technical Information Service, Springfield, Va. Report PB91-137240. 38pp.

Lazcana-Barrero, M.A., and J.M. Packard. 1989. The occurrence of manatees (*Trichechus manatus*) in Tamaulipas, Mexico. *Marine Mammal Science* 5(2):202–205.

Mou Sue, L.L., et al. 1990. Distribution and status of manatees (*Trichechus manatus*) in Panama. *Marine Mammal Science* 6(3):234–241.

O'Shea, T.J., and C.A. Salisbury. In press. Belize—a last stronghold for manatees in the Caribbean. *Oryx.*

Powell, J.A. 1978. Evidence of carnivory in manatees (*Trichechus manatus*). *Journal of Mammalogy* 59:442.

Powell, J.A., D.W. Belitsky and G.B. Rathbun. 1981. Status of the West Indian manatee (*Trichechus manatus*) in Puerto Rico. *Journal of Mammalogy* 62:642–646.

Rathbun, G.B., J.A. Powell and G. Cruz. 1983. Status of the West Indian manatee in Honduras. *Biological Conservation* 26:301–308.

Rathbun, G.B., et al. 1985. The distribution of manatees and sea turtles in Puerto Rico. National Technical Information Service, Springfield, Va., Rept. PB86–1518347AS.

Rathbun, G.B., C.A. Woods and J.A. Ottenwalder. 1985. The manatee in Haiti. *Oryx* 19:234–236.

The West African Manatee

Husar, S.L. 1978. *Trichechus senegalensis. Mammalian Species* No. 89.

Nishiwaki, M., et al. 1982. Recent survey on the distribution of the West African manatee. Scientific reports of the Whales Research Institute, no. 34:137–147.

Poche, R. 1973. Niger's threatened Park W. *Oryx* 12:216–222.

Powell, J.A. (unpub.) Manatees in the Gambia River basin and potential impact of Balingho antisalt dam with notes on Ivory Coast, West Africa. A Trip Report.

Reeves, R.R., D. Tuboku-Metzger and R.A. Kapindi. 1988. Distribution and exploitation of manatees in Sierra Leone. *Oryx* 22(2):75–84.

Sykes, S. 1974. How to save the mermaids. *Oryx* 12(4):465–470.

The Amazonian Manatee

Best, R.C. 1982. Seasonal breeding in the Amazonian manatee, *Trichechus inunguis* (Mammalia: Sirenia). *Biotropica* 14(1):76–78.

————. 1983. Apparent dry-season fasting in Amazonian manatees (Mammalia: Sirenia). *Biotropica* 15(1):61–64.

Best, R.C., and W.E. Magnusson. 1979. Status report of the Amazonian manatee project 1975–1979. Submitted to Instituto Nacional de Pesquisas da Amazonia, Manaus, Brazil.

Best, R.C., et al. 1982. Artificial feeding for unweaned Amazonian manatees. *International Zoo Yearbook* 22:263–267.

Gallivan, G.J., and R.C. Best. 1980. Metabolism and respiration of the Amazonian manatee (*Trichechus inunguis*). *Physiological Zoology* 53(3):245–253.

Gallivan, G.J., and R.C. Best. 1986. The influence of feeding and fasting on the metabolic rate and ventilation of the Amazonian manatee (*Trichechus inunguis*). *Physiological Zoology* 59(5):552–557.

Gallivan, G.J., R.C. Best and J.W. Kanwisher. 1983. Temperature regulation in the Amazonian manatee (*Trichechus inunguis*). *Physiological Zoology* 56(2):255–262.

Husar, S.L. 1977. *Trichechus inunguis. Mammalian Species* no. 72:4pp.

Myers, N. 1986. *Tropical Deforestation and a Mega-Extinction Spasm.* pp. 394–409. *Conservation Biology*, ed. M.E. Soule. Sunderland, Ma.: Sinauer Associates, Inc.

Timm, R.M., L. Albuja V. and B.L. Clauson. 1986. Ecology, distribution, harvest, and conservation of the Amazonian manatee *Trichechus inunguis* in Ecuador. *Biotropica* 18(2):150–156.

The Dugong

Bayliss, P. and W.J. Freeland 1989. Seasonal distribution and abundance of dugongs in the western Gulf of Carpentaria. *Australian Journal of Wildlife Research* 16:141–149.

Heinsohn, G.E., H. Marsh and A.V. Spain. 1976. Extreme risk of mortality to dugongs (Mammalia: Sirenia) from netting operations. *Australian Journal of Wildlife Research* 3:117–121.

Husar, S.L. 1978. *Dugong dugon. Mammalian Species* No. 88:7pp.

Marsh, H., ed. 1981. *The Dugong.* Proceedings of a seminar/workshop held May 8–13, 1979 at James Cook University of North Queensland, Townsville, Australia.

————. 1988. An ecological basis for dugong conservation in Australia. pp. 9–21. *Marine mammals of Australasia: Field Biology and Captive Management,* ed. M.L. Augee. New South Wales: Mosman, The Royal Society.

Marsh, H., G.E. Heinsohn and L.M. Marsh. 1984. Breeding cycle, life history and population dynamics of the dugong, *Dugong dugon* (Sirenia: Dugongidae). *Australian Journal of Zoology* 32:767–788.

Marsh, H., A.V. Spain and G.E. Heinsohn. 1978. Physiology of the dugong. *Comparative Biochemistry and Physiology*, Part A, 61(2):159–162.

Nishiwaki, M., and H. Marsh. 1985. Dugong Dugong dugon (Müller, 1776). pp. 1–31. Handbook of Marine Mammals, eds. S.H. Ridgway and R. Harrison, vol. 3. The Sirenians and Baleen Whales. New York: Academic Press.

Smith, A., and H. Marsh. 1990. Management of traditional hunting of dugongs [*Dugong dugon* (Müller, 1976)] in the northern Great Barrier Reef, Australia. *Environmental Management* 14(1):47–55.

Steller's Sea Cow: A Story of Human Negligence

Brandt, J.F. 1849. Contributions to sirenology, being principally an illustrated natural history of *Rhytina*. 122pp. Translated in 1974 by A. Barlow. Available from National Technical Information Service, Springfield, Va.

Domning, D.P. 1978. Sirenian evolution in the North Pacific Ocean. University of California Publications in Geological Sciences. University of California Press, Berkeley. Volume 118. 176pp + plates.

———. 1987. Sea cow family reunion. *Natural History* 96:64–70.

Domning, D.P., and T.A. Deméré. 1984. New material of *Hydrodamalis cuestae* (Mammalia: Dugongidae) from the Miocene and Pliocene of San Diego County, California. *Transactions of the San Diego Society of Natural History* 20(12):169–188.

Scheffer, V.B. 1972. The weight of the Steller sea cow. *Journal of Mammalogy* 53(4):912–914.

———. 1973. The last days of the sea cow. *Smithsonian* 3:64–67.

Stejneger, L. 1887. How the great northern sea–cow (*Rytina*) became exterminated. *The American Naturalist* 21(12):1047–1054.

Takahashi, S., D.P. Domning and T. Saito. 1986. *Dusisiren dewana*, N.Sp. (Mammalia: Sirenia), a new ancestor of Steller's sea cow from the Upper Miocene of Yamagata prefecture, northeastern Japan. *Transactions and Proceedings of the Paleontological Society of Japan* No. 141:296–321.

Conservation

Anonymous. 1987. Keys to Florida's future: winning in a competitive world. Final report of the state comprehensive planning committee. Available through Florida Department of Community Affairs, Tallahassee, Florida.

Haddad, K.D., and B.A. Hoffman. 1986. Charlotte Harbor habitat assessment. pp. 176–192. *Proceedings of the conference: Managing cumulative effects in Florida wetlands*, eds. E.D. Estevez et al. October 1985, Sarasota, Florida. New College Environmental Studies Program Publication No. 37. Omnipress, Madison, Wisconsin.

Holt, S.J., and L.M. Talbot. 1978. New principles for the conservation of wild living resources. *Wildlife Monographs* 43(2):6–33.

Leatherwood, S., and R.R. Reeves, eds. 1989. Marine mammal research and conservation in Sri Lanka, 1985–1986. Nairobi, Kenya. United Nations Environment Programme, Marine Mammal Technical Report No. 1.

Lewis, R.R. III. 1986. Marine wetland loss in Tampa Bay and management restoration recommendations. pp. 159–174. *Proceedings of the Conference: Managing Cumulative Effects in Florida Wetlands*, eds. E.D. Estevez et al. October 1985, Sarasota, Florida. New College Environmental Studies Program Publication no. 37, Omnipress, Madison, Wisconsin.

Marine Mammal Commission. 1988. Preliminary assessment of habitat protection needs for West Indian manatees on the east coast of Florida and Georgia. Available from Marine Mammal Commission, Washington, D.C.

———. 1989. Annual report of the Marine Mammal Commission, calendar year 1989. A report to Congress.

Reynolds, J.E. III, and C.J. Gluckman. 1988. Protection of West Indian manatees (*Trichechus manatus*) in Florida. Final report to Marine Mammal Commission. National Technical Information Service, Springfield, Va., Report PB88–222922.

Reynolds, J.E. III, and K.D. Haddad, eds. 1990. Report of the workshop on geographic information systems as an aid to managing habitat for West Indian manatees in Florida and Georgia. Florida Marine Research Publication no. 49.

Simberloff, D. 1985. Design of nature reserves. pp. 315–338. *Wildlife Conservation Evaluation*, ed. M.B. Usher. New York: Chapman and Hall.

U.S. Fish and Wildlife Service. 1989. Florida manatee (*Trichechus manatus latirostris*) recovery plan. Prep. by the Florida manatee recovery team for the U.S. Fish and Wildlife Service, Atlanta, Georgia.

INDEX

Italic numbers indicate illustrations